PYTHAGORAS, THE MASTER

ALSO BY CAROL DUNN
FROM LINDISFARNE BOOKS

Plato's Dialogues: Path to Initiation (2015)

PYTHAGORAS

THE MASTER

PHILOLAUS, PRESOCRATIC FOLLOWER

CAROL DUNN

LINDISFARNE BOOKS | 2018

Lindisfarne Books

An imprint of SteinerBooks / Anthroposophic Press, Inc.
610 Main St., Great Barrington, MA 01230
www.steinerbooks.org

Cover image: *Pythagoras* by John August Knapp (1853–1938)
Design: Jens Jensen

Harmony of the Spheres by Joscelyn Godwin, published by Inner
Traditions International and Bear *&* Company, ©1992. All rights reserved.
www.InnerTraditions.com. Reprinted with permission of publisher.

Philolaus of Croton: Pythagorean and Presocratic by Carl A. Huffman,
published by Cambridge University © 1993. All rights reserved.
www.cambridge.org. Reprinted with pending permission of publisher.

Pythagoras and the Pythagoreans: A Brief History by Charles Kahn,
published by Hackett Publishing © 1993. All rights reserved.
www.hackettpublishing.com. Reprinted with pending permission of
publisher.

Printed in the United States of America

LIBRARY OF CONGRESS CONTROL NUMBER: 2017954832

ISBN: 978-1-58420-948-5 (paperback)
ISBN: 978-1-58420-949-2 (eBook)

CHAPTER 1

PYTHAGORAS, THE MASTER

Pythagoras was one of the greatest geniuses the West has ever produced, and yet, apart from his famous Pythagorean theorem, he is practically unknown. And if we rely on modern scholars and academics we will find that his long-forgotten legacy is misunderstood, even distorted, and is therefore, almost nonexistent.

How *have* Western academics construed Pythagoras? The renowned historian of philosophy, W. K. C. Guthrie, points out in his book *The History of Philosophy* (vol. 1, 146) that because of the lack of evidentiary material it is difficult to get a clear picture of Pythagorean developments before Plato. He states: "This pre-Platonic Pythagoreanism can, to a large extent, be regarded as a unity. We shall note developments...as and when we can, but it would be unwise to hope that...in the fragmentary state of our knowledge, these are sufficiently distinguishable chronologically to allow for separate treatment of earlier and later phases. The best course will be that which Aristotle himself felt forced to adopt before the end of the fourth century BC; on the whole he regards the ideas of all previous generations of Pythagoreans as sufficiently homogeneous to be spoken of together, but in his general treatment he sometimes refers to 'all' when he criticizes a tenet which he confines to 'some' of the school or to a named individual within it." Guthrie reveals two of the major sticking points in Pythagorean inquiry.

The first is that Guthrie has defined himself as one following Aristotle in his philosophical deliberations on Pythagoras. The second, following Aristotle, is his view that all generations of Pythagoreans before

Plato were to be regarded as a homogeneity. The assumption here is that before Plato no particular Pythagorean doctrine could be trusted, and since Guthrie has identified himself as an Aristotelian, we may assume he will also favor Aristotle over Plato in his conclusions. This is the third major sticking point in Western philosophy: the divide between Plato's metaphysical worldview and Aristotle's scientific worldview. We shall see how this plays out over the centuries in the West.

Moving ahead to the work of Charles H. Kahn—*Pythagoras and the Pythagoreans: A Brief History,* he reminds us that there are "three lives of Pythagoras from late antiquity, by Diogenes Laertius, Porphyry, and Iamblichus, in that order." In these works, Kahn says: "Pythagoras is described as something more than human, as the god Apollo in human form. A golden thigh and the gift of bilocation confirmed his supernatural status: he was seen in Croton and Metapontum at the same time.... Above all, Pythagoras could recall his previous incarnations, including the Trojan hero Euphorbus mentioned in Homer. His learning was universal. He first studied geometry and astronomy with Anaximander, then hieroglyphic symbolism with the priests of Egypt and the science of dreams with Hebrew masters...He studied also with the Arabs, with the Chaldeans of Babylon, and finally with Zoroaster, who taught him the ritual of purification and the nature of things. In the late tradition Pythagoras' life assumes mythic form; he becomes the paradigm of the *theos aner,* the "divine human" who absorbs all forms of wisdom in order to become a sage, a seer, a teacher, and a benefactor of the human race.... And the formation of this legendary picture begins very early. The story of Pythagoras' studies with the priests of Egypt is mentioned by Isocrates in the early fourth century BC and hinted at even earlier by Herodotus" (Kahn, 6).

Kahn tells us,

Pythagoras, son of Mnesarchus, was born on the island of Samos sometime in the middle of the sixth century BC. He came to maturity then just as the earliest Greek science and natural philosophy was developing in Miletus, on the nearby coast of Asia Minor. This synchronism is significant. Pythagoras was a contemporary of Anaximenes and Xenophanes, and if he had any contact at all with the new science it would have been a cosmology of the Milesian type that was familiar to him. Like Xenophanes, Pythagoras left Ionia and settled in southern Italy in the latter half of the sixth century. We know nothing of his life before his arrival in Croton, in approximately 530 BC. (Kahn, 6)

Kahn refers to the nineteenth-century historian of philosophy, Edward Zeller, who had recognized that there was another side to Pythagoras—namely that he was known above all for his teaching of immortality and reincarnation. Kahn continues, "Zeller was skeptical in regard to Pythagoras' scientific achievements, and his skepticism has been reinforced by the critical work of several more recent scholars. The most extreme judgment was that of Erich Frank who claimed that 'all the discoveries attributed to Pythagoras himself or his disciples by later writers were really the achievement of certain Italian mathematicians of Plato's time,' a full century later than Pythagoras" (Kahn, 2).

Walter Burkert reached a far more moderate conclusion, though leaning in the same direction, in his monumental study *Weisheit and Wissenschaft* (1962, revised translation into English, 1972), which has transformed our understanding of the ancient traditions surrounding Pythagoras and his school. Burkert traces the Pythagorean cosmology and number philosophy—reported by Aristotle—back to Philolaus in the middle or late fifth century, but he finds no evidence connecting it to the founder of the school. Pythagoras himself, on Burkert's view, is a shamanistic figure, a charismatic spiritual leader and organizer (like Moses perhaps) who exercised a great influence on the civic life of Magna Graecia, but who contributed nothing to mathematics or philosophy. In fact Burkert claims that all of Pythagoras' theories hearkened from Plato's time and were reflected back upon Pythagoras, making it *appear* that they originated from a pre-Platonic time. Kahn appears to believe Burkert, whom he says "has conclusively shown that the conception of Pythagorean philosophy that is taken for granted in later antiquity is essentially the work of Plato and his immediate disciples" (Kahn, 3).

Kahn also investigates Pythagorean philosophy before Plato in chapter 3, and there he states, "Since Pythagoras and his earliest disciples left behind no written record of their teaching, the history of Pythagorean philosophy must begin with the first known Pythagorean book. This is the work of Philolaus in the last half of the fifth century BC" (Kahn, 23). He adds:

> Burkert's results have been confirmed and extended by Carl Huffman's careful analysis of the fragments and testimonia in the context of the development of cosmological theories in the fifth century. These fragments reflect essentially the same worldview that is attributed to the Pythagoreans by Aristotle and ascribed to Philolaus and the Pythagoreans in the later doxography deriving from Theophrastus. *So it will be convenient to refer to this, the oldest attested version of Pythagorean theory, as the system of Philolaus, without prejudging the question of its originality.* (Kahn, 23)

Kahn thus reveals a fourth major sticking point in Pythagorean inquiry: namely was Philolaus the author of Pythagorean doctrines—as Burkert suggests?

Later, in chapter 3, Kahn states, "First we must deal with the problem in the interpretation of Philolaus' cosmology.... Aristotle reports that for the Pythagoreans 'all things are numbers' or 'imitate numbers' or 'resemble numbers.' What corresponds to this in the literal quotations from Philolaus is the claim that 'all things which are known have number' (fr.4), hence the process by which the cosmos came into existence seems to have been conceived as analogous to a generation of the numbers" (Kahn, 27). "The first thing harmoniously fitted together, the one in the center of the sphere, is called Hestia, the hearth" (fr.7).

"My account," says Kahn, follows Aristotle in assuming that the Pythagoreans generate the heavens by the same process that generates the natural numbers, so that "the one in the center of the sphere" is both the central fire, or Hearth and also the first integer. Thus Aristotle reports that the Pythagoreans "construct the whole heavens out of numbers, but not out of monads, for they assume that monads have magnitude" (Met.1080b18). This interpretation has been challenged by Huffman, who claims that Philolaus did not confuse things with numbers but that it was Aristotle (in his rather uncharitable interpretation) who attributed this confusion to the Pythagoreans.

On Huffman's reading of fragment 5, things "signify" or "point to" (*semainei*) the forms of number. Hence the central fire points to the number one but is not identical with it. It is, Huffman claims, "impossible to imagine that he [Philolaus] confused the arithmetical unit with the central fire. For if he did, his arithmetical unit is more than a bare monad with position; it is also fiery and orbited by ten bodies" (Huffman, 205).

Kahn asks, "Is Aristotle mistaken when he reports that the Pythagoreans generate the physical universe out of numbers? He replies that the texts of Philolaus are too few and fragmentary for us to be sure." He adds: "Although it is always risky to rely on Aristotle's report of his predecessors' views when we cannot confirm this report with original texts.... I am inclined to accept Aristotle's account of this numerical cosmology, despite Huffman's doubts" (Kahn, 28).

"Scientific evaluations of the system of Philolaus have been very diverse. Since no explanation is provided for the retrograde motion of the planets, and since the theory posits a central fire and a counter-earth that have no observable consequences." Burkert charged that this was not scientific astronomy but rather "mythology in scientific clothing."

Huffman on the other hand, describes the system of Philolaus as "the most impressive example of Presocratic speculative astronomy" and "a much more coherent model of the cosmos" than that of any other fifth-century thinker. Although Huffman recognizes that Philolaus shows *little interest in identifying physical causes or explaining celestial machinery,* he insists that this system is "on a par with the rest of Presocratic astronomy in accounting for phenomena and that he may even have been ahead of his contemporaries in assigning the correct relative positions to the planets.... Philolaus produces an elegant astronomical model, constructed according to mathematical principles of number and order" (Huffman, 29–30).

Kahn concludes "Such praise may seem excessive for a system that is after all, very strange. But we must remember that Philolaus and his Pythagorean colleagues were speculating in an age of breathtaking intellectual exploration, when the atomists were elaborating a world picture that would eventually serve as the starting point for modern physical theory, but which was created with scarcely a shred of empirical evidence, on the basis of a priori, metaphysical considerations alone. Just as the atomists by their speculative imagination anticipate the mechanistic worldview, so do the Pythagoreans anticipate the mathematical interpretation of nature" (Kahn, 30).

Huffman himself states in the preface of his book, "Since Philolaus is, in my opinion, the foremost of the early Pythagoreans, this book should give a good picture of the dominant themes of fifth-century Pythagoreanism. However, it is not intended as a comprehensive study of fifth-century Pythagoreanism and has little to say about Pythagoras himself, largely because the relationship between Pythagoras and Philolaus belongs almost totally to the realm of conjecture" (Huffman, xiii).

To show how widespread is the philosophical refutation of Pythagoras, let us conclude with a few comments by respected twentieth century philosophers. For example, in his book, *Early Greek Philosophy,* John Burnet states: "It is not till later, when Egyptian priests and Alexandrian Jews began to vie with one another in discovering the sources of Greek philosophy in their own past, that we have definite statements to the effect that it came from Phoenicia or Egypt. But the so-called Egyptian philosophy was only arrived at by a process of turning primitive myths into allegories" (Burnet, 16).

Later on he says: "Now we know of no Greek, in the times we are dealing with, who could read an Egyptian book or even listen to the discourse of an Egyptian priest, and we never hear until a later date of Oriental teachers who wrote or spoke in Greek...It is impossible to conceive of philosophical ideas being communicated through an uneducated dragoman...It is not worthwhile to ask whether the communication of philosophical ideas was possible or not, till some evidence has been produced that any of these peoples *had* a philosophy to communicate" (Burnet, 18–19).

As for Guthrie, he states, "It was both as religious teacher and as scientific genius that he was from his own lifetime and for many centuries afterward venerated by his followers...The attempts to minimize one or the other side of his nature arise from the difficulty which a modern mind experiences in reconciling adherence to a comparatively primitive set of religious and superstitious beliefs with the rational pursuit of mathematical science and cosmic speculation" (Guthrie, 181). To show how far afield Western investigators can wander, another example from Guthrie will suffice. He says, "The ban (on eating beans) was also rationalized in a political sense. It was said to symbolize the oligarchic tendencies of Pythagoras, since beans were used as counters in the Democratic process of election by lot" (ibid., 184–185). Reading such a sentence, one must roll one's eyes to heaven, since Guthrie had stated in his own work (page 175) that Pythagoras' motive for acquiring power "was not personal ambition, but a zeal for reforming society (according to his own moral ideas.... There is no reason to doubt the general statement which we find in Diogenes Laertius, in his book *Lives of the Eminent Philosophers* (viii, 3), that he gave the Italians the Constitution and with his followers governed the state so well that it deserved the name of *aristocracy* ('government of the best') in its literal sense."

Moreover, F. M. Cornford wrote in his book *From Religion to Philosophy:*

> The words *Religion* and *Philosophy,* perhaps suggest to most people two distinct provinces of thought, between which, if (like the Greeks) we include Science under Philosophy, there is commonly held to be some sort of border warfare. It is however, also possible to think of them as successive phases, or modes, of the expression of man's feelings and beliefs about the world.... The modes of thought that attain clear definition and explicit statement in philosophy were already implicit in the unreasoned intuitions of mythology. For our guide we take the theorem, maintained by the new French school of sociologists, that the key to religious representation lies in the social structure of the community which elaborates it.... Pythagoras seems to have held to the conception of a group soul, incarnate in himself, but living on after his death as the Logos of his disciples. (Cornford, v and 203)

To put it bluntly, most of these comments would have been seen by Pythagoras himself as pure nonsense!

ARISTOTLE

We cannot conclude this introduction to Pythagoras without discussing Aristotle—the great Aristotle! So overwhelming has been his influence been on Western civilization that my impression of him is one of a vast canopy of scientific, philosophical, and classificatory knowledge that stretches unbroken from the fourth century BC right into the twenty-first century. As we have seen, it is Aristotle's worldview that has been accepted and confirmed by the majority of modern academics we have quoted. Aristotle is not a man to be trifled with. This fact assumes even more importance when we consider that the majority of Western philosophers, historians, philosophers of science, and scholars down the ages, have held Aristotle, in general, to be the pole star of their own worldview.

Before noting Aristotle's critical views about Pythagoras (or the *Pythagoreans*, as he liked to call them), let us recall Guthrie's comment:

> Aristotle is the earliest author to give any detailed information about the Pythagoreans, and in trying to recover their views up to the time of Plato it will be necessary to pay the closest attention to what he says. Of Pythagoras himself as a writer we have only the contradictory statements of much later men, some of whom say he wrote nothing, while others claim to give the names of some of his books. Knowing the tendency of the school to attribute all its works to the founder, we will treat these claims with well merited suspicion. We have no fragments of Pythagorean writings before the time of Philolaus, the leader of the school at Thebes at the end of the fifth century, who is mentioned in Plato's *Phaedo*. [However, Guthrie concedes,] When we come to the "fragments" of Aristotle, it is advisable to be cautious, since most are not represented as his actual words, and some in late compilers are doubtless at second or third hand. (Guthrie, *History of Greek Philosophy,* vol. 1, 154)

Sir Thomas Heath sounds another note of caution in *Aristarchus: The Ancient Copernican:* "Aristotle... while making historical surveys of the doctrines of his predecessors a regular preliminary to the statement of his own, discusses them too much from the point of view of his own system; often misrepresenting them for the purposes of making a controversial point or finding support for some particular thesis" (p. 1).

Two final comments by Guthrie might be quite revealing:

> As for Aristotle, the only safe conclusion to draw from his silence (about Pythagorean mathematics) is that he hesitated to write of Pythagoras at all, preferring to speak generally of Pythagoreans because Pythagoras had already become a legend and his critical mind could not feel satisfied that any specific doctrine was to be traced with certainty to the Master himself. Once we speak of the Pythagoreans however, it might equally well be argued that by Aristotle's time at least, they had become a purely scientific school, since it is only as such that they appear in his extant treaties. This argument has in fact been used, but is of little weight. The simple answer is that only their mathematics and philosophy were relevant to Aristotle's subject matter in his extant treaties. (ibid., 168)

As far as their doctrines are concerned, Guthrie offers the following:

> [The Pythagoreans] are the kind of men who claimed to have made the tremendous discovery that the world of nature was constructed on a mathematical plan. It need cause not surprise us that they express this by saying at one time that *things were numbers* and at another that they existed by *mimesis* of numbers. To Aristotle, with his instinct for rational classification and the contempt for religious or superstitious ways of thinking which went naturally with a newly won emancipation from them, it was all exasperatingly illogical. The modern scholar or scientist—views it more sympathetically. (ibid., 231)

As to statements made by Aristotle himself, let us reflect on his view of first principles, outlined in *Physics* (203a 1–10). He says, "...all physical philosophers of repute have discussed the *apeiron* (unlimited) and all have treated it as a first principle. Some, as for example the Pythagoreans and Plato, regard it as a first principle per se and itself a substance, not an attribute of some other thing. But the Pythagoreans regard it as present in sensibles: for them, number is not a separate substance" (Philip, 64).

The first part of this quotation says that all physical philosophers have dealt with the *apeiron,* the unlimited, as a first principle. (But neither Pythagoras nor Plato is a physical philosopher. They represent the metaphysical worldview). Then he says that the Pythagoreans and Plato regard it as a first principle per se—not an attribute in some other thing. Lastly he says that the Pythagoreans regard the apeiron as present *in* sensibles, number is not a separate substance. These statements, taken together, show a great ambivalence on the part of Aristotle. On the one hand he accuses the Pythagoreans of positing that the apeiron is a transcendental principle, but then judges that they regard it as present in sensibles.

His understanding of Pythagorean number is equally opaque. He does not understand that mathematics is a language by which to *describe* the universe. Even his scientific worldview fails him, when he assumes that for Pythagoreans numbers are in sensibles. He makes no mention of Pythagoras' originating, transcendental principle because, even though it was rumored, he rejected it.

In *Metaphysics* (bk I, ch. 5, 986a 17), he makes a most succinct and yet all-encompassing analysis of the worldview of the "so-called Pythagoreans": "They hold that the elements of number are the even and the odd, and that of these the latter is limited, and the former unlimited, and that the One proceeds from both of these (for it is both even and odd) and number from the One; and that the whole heaven, as has been said, is numbers" (McKeon, 699).

In this case Aristotle creates yet another confusion. He conflates the idea of number—the even and the odd, and hypothesizes without evidence that the odd is limited and the even is unlimited. Since the Pythagorean originating Monad is a single transcendental principle symbolizing God, it would be difficult to imagine it being designated as limited, as Aristotle suggests. Aristotle has hypothesized that for the Pythagoreans there are two originating material principles of our cosmos, and then posits that the One proceeds *from* these (it is both even and odd). In my view this passage represents a turning upside-down of Pythagoras' principles. For him there is only the Monad, God, as originating principle.

Aristotle continues in *Metaphysics* (bk. 1, ch. 5, 987a 15) as follows: "The Pythagoreans have said...there are two principles, but added this much, which is peculiar to them, that they thought that finitude and infinity were not attributes of certain other things (e.g., of fire, earth, or anything else of this kind), but that infinity itself and unity itself were the substances of things of which they are predicated. This is why number was the substance of all things" (McKeon, 700). Again, this would appear to posit that the realm of numbers constitutes the entire focus of Pythagoras' doctrines, whereas for the Master himself number was the mathematical language by which to describe the cosmos. This does not downplay the importance of number, but Pythagoras used number as a tool—the central focus was on describing our cosmos.

The next Aristotelian hypothesis is prefaced by Kahn, who states, "My account follows Aristotle in assuming the Pythagoreans generate the heavens by the same process that generates the natural numbers, so that for Philolaus 'the one in the center of the sphere' is both the central fire, or hearth and also the first integer." Thus Aristotle reports that the Pythagoreans "construct the whole heavens out of numbers, but not monads, for they assume that monads have magnitude" (*Meta.* 1080b 18). This interpretation has been challenged by Huffman who claims that Philolaus did not confuse things with numbers but that it was Aristotle (in his rather uncharitable interpretation) who attributed this confusion to the Pythagoreans.

On Huffman's reading of fragment 5, things "signify" or "point to" (*semainei*) the forms of number. Hence the central fire points to the number one, but is not identical with it. It is, Huffman claims, "impossible to imagine that he [Philolaus] confused the arithmetical unit with the central fire. For if he did his arithmetical unit is more than a bare monad with position, it is also fiery and orbited by ten bodies" (Huffman 205). Again Aristotle reveals his confusion about Pythagorean number. And, we would note Huffman's disagreement with Aristotle reveals, once again, that neither of them possessed the metaphysical doctrine of Pythagoras that the Monad, God, is transcendental and therefore does not have magnitude.

Of the many examples given here of Aristotle's bafflement regarding Pythagoras, the one regarding his cosmology is most vexing. Guthrie tells us *"The most remarkable feature of the Pythagorean cosmology recorded by Aristotle is that it displaced the Earth from the center of the universe and made it into a planet circling the center like the others.* This idea was unparalleled in pre-Platonic thought, and called for a bold leap of the scientific imagination which proved too much for Plato himself. It was not, however, an anticipation of the heliocentric theory, even if it be right to say with Burnet that 'the identification of the central fire with the Sun was a detail in comparison with setting the Earth to revolve in an orbit'" (Guthrie, 282).

It is not surprising that Aristotle could not understand or appreciate the heliocentric theory, which was not scientifically rediscovered until the time of Newton and Kepler, who more than any other scientist delved most deeply into the scientific inspiration of Pythagoras, as well as to Philolaus. However, undoubtedly during Aristotle's time a rumor of the heliocentric theory did float about and *was* attributed to the "Pythagoreans" rather than Pythagoras himself.

Copernicus—vexed by the "theories of homocentric spheres of Eudoxus" and rival theories of "eccentrics and epicycles"—turned to the ancient philosophers to see what theories they might have about the motion of the Earth. "He found that Cicero attributed a belief in the motion of the Earth to one Hicetas, and that similar statements were made by Plutarch about Philolaus, Ecphantus, and Heraclides of Pontus.... He makes them the point of departure for his own exploration of the problem" (Armitage, *Copernicus*, 70–71). In the seventeenth century, the heliocentric theory was rediscovered by Copernicus, affirmed by Galileo, finalized in its official form by Kepler, and used as a point of departure for the theory of gravitation of Isaac Newton, as we shall see later on.

Even Heath, who has served as a most reliable chronicler of Pythagoras' astonishing achievements could not believe that he had discovered the heliocentric theory because he still believed that for Pythagoras, Earth was the center of the cosmos. Such was the confusion of belief and disbelief even up to the twentieth century and beyond.

Here Guthrie, too, was proven wrong, for he concedes: "Looking back, it seems as if it was Aristotle who was leading science on to the wrong track. Today the scientific description of everything in the physical world takes the form of numerical equations.... For this reason, a historian of science has claimed that Pythagoras' discovery changed the whole course of history" (Guthrie, 238). It is disappointing that Guthrie did not give that brave soul a name.

Lest we think the onslaughts against Pythagoras are concluded, there are more, and they hail from a predictable direction. Since so little evidence of ancient Greece has remained to this day, one would assume that a highly respected Western scholar such as Guthrie would have referred more to the accounts of the famous philosophers supplied by Diogenes Laertius. However, critically, where Laertius gives some detail of Pythagoras' sacred expeditions in Egypt and elsewhere, Guthrie has excluded such information in his version of Pythagoras' life, except as the merest passing reference (Guthrie, 173).

In hindsight, one might suggest that Western rational scholars, wedded as they later became to the scientific Aristotelian worldview, were by nature, or by Aristotelian persuasion, loath to touch the idea of religion, the ancient mysteries, or enlightenment. Since most Western academics have been overwhelmingly influenced by Aristotle, one might conclude that the Western tradition in philosophy and science has been somewhat insular, and reveals a lack of willingness to investigate other civilizations and cultures, especially if they stretch into the mists of time — so sure are they that Western values and the scientific version of history are far superior to anything that had come before.

This situation is emphasized to a considerable degree when we consider that many of the same philosophers have been very willing to troll the doxographic tradition for confirmation of their researches. Thomas Heath reminds us that the meaning of doxographic is that statements made under that rubric are not necessarily reliable. He continues: "Most important for our purposes are the notices in the *Doxographi Graeci*, collected by Diehls. The main source from which these retailers of the opinions of philosophers drew, directly or indirectly, was the great work of Theophrastus, the successor of Aristotle, entitled *Physical Opinions*" (Heath, *Aristarchus of Samos*, 2).

Heath concludes: "To show at a glance the conclusions of [Hermann] Diels as to the relation of the various representatives of the doxographic and biographic traditions to one another and to the original sources, I append a genealogical table":

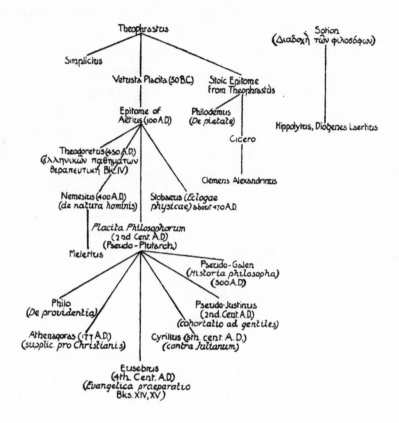

Genealogical Table, in Heath, Aristarchus of Samos, *p. 3*

As we can see, the doxographic tradition is so heavily weighted as to almost sideline the biographical tradition into silence. We note only Sotion, Hippolytus and Diogenes Laertius are included as biographers, whereas stemming from Theophrastus, there are a veritable plethora of well known names, including Simplicius, Aetius, Clemens of Alexandria, Stobaeus, Pseudo-Plutarch, Pseudo Galen, Philo, Athenagoras and Eusebius.

Let me underscore that when we see Theophrastus at the apex of the genealogical table of doxography, we must automatically infer he is passing on the received wisdom of his teacher, Aristotle. And, as I have pointed out, Aristotle's vast canopy of influence lasts up to the present day.

One cannot ignore the fact that as Western civilization evolved, it took the turn into a scientific inquiry of all disciplines. And, perhaps it was intended to be so. But, the wholesale substitution of Aristotelian scientific investigation for Platonic metaphysics still infects the whole of Western civilization. Indeed, it reveals itself as biased. It is because of that movement into science—divorced from the transcendental—that modern interpreters are either unable or unwilling to accurately locate or honor the remarkable contributions of Pythagoras to Western science and civilization.

But such is not the case concerning the biographer, Diogenes Laertius. In writing *Lives of the Eminent Philosophers* in the third century AD, he began by reviewing the Milesian school of philosophers, and afterward states:

> Let us proceed to examine the philosophy of Italy which was started by Pythagoras, son of the gem engraver Mnesarchus, according to Hermippus, a Samian (meaning from the island of Samos). Some indeed say that he was descended through Euthyphro, Hippasus and Marmacus from Cleonymus, who was exiled from Phlius...from Samos he went, it is said to Lesbos with an introduction to Pherecydes from his uncle Zoilus.... He was a pupil, as already stated, of Pherecydes of Syros, after whose death he went to Samos to be the pupil of Hermodamas, Creophylus' descendent, a man already advanced in years. While still young, so eager was he for knowledge, he left his own country and had himself initiated into all the mysteries and rites not only of Greece but also of foreign countries. Now he was in Egypt when Polycrates (the tyrant) sent him a letter of introduction to Amasis (the Pharoah of Egypt); he learnt the Egyptian language, so we learn from Antiphon in his book *On Men of Outstanding Merit,* and he also journeyed among the Chaldeans and the Magi. Then while in Crete he went down into the cave of Ida with Epimenides; he also entered the Egyptian sanctuaries, and was told the secret law concerning the gods. After that he returned to Samos to find his country under the tyranny of Polycrates; so he sailed away to Croton in Italy, and there he lay down a constitution for the Italian Greeks, and he and his followers were held in great estimation; for being

nearly 300 in number, so well did they govern the state that its Constitution was in effect a true aristocracy (government by the best).

This is what Heraclides of Pontus tells us he used to say about himself: that he had once been Aethalides and was accounted to be Hermes' son and Hermes told him he might choose any gift he liked except immortality; so he asked to retain through life and through death a memory of his experiences. Hence in his life he could record everything, and when he died he still retained the same memories. (Laertius, 325)

Afterward, in course of time, his soul entered Euphorbus and he was wounded by Menelaus. Now Euphorbus used to say that he had once been Aethalides and obtained this gift from Hermes. When Euphorbus died, his soul passed into Hermotimus, and he also, wishing to authenticate the story, went up to the temple of Apollo at Branchidae, where he identified the shield which Menelaus, on his voyage home from Troy, had dedicated to Apollo, so he said: the shield, now so rotten through and through, that the ivory facing only was left. When Hermotimus died, he became Pyrrhus, a fisherman of Delos, and again he remembered everything, how he was Aethalides, then Euphorbus, then Hermotimus, then Pyrrhus. But when Pyrrhus died, he became Pythagoras, and still remembered all the facts mentioned (ibid.).

Laertius continues, "There are some who insist, absurdly enough, that Pythagoras left no writings whatever. Pythagoras in fact wrote three books, *On Education, On Statesmanship, and On Nature.* But the book which passes as the work of Pythagoras is by Lysis of Tarentum, a Pythagorean, who fled to Thebes and taught Epaminondas" (ibid., 327).

As we can see, Laertius adds important biographical details of Pythagoras' life. And, from his "mere biography," I bring to your attention a most remarkable passage! In fact, I would venture to suggest that it may be the most important passage to be found in all of Diogenes Laertius' compilations. The passage in question is attributed to Alexander Polyhistor, a respected first century BC philosopher and mathematician. In my view it amounts to a template, and a synoptic statement of Pythagoras' worldview and cosmology! Laertius states:

Alexander in his *Successions of Philosophers* says he found in the Pythagorean memoirs, the following tenets as well: "The principle of all things is the monad or unit; arising from this monad the undefined dyad, or two, serves as material substratum, which is cause; from the monad and the undefined dyad spring numbers; from numbers, points; from points, lines; from lines, plane figures; from plane figures, solid figures; from solid figures, sensible bodies, the elements of which are four: fire, water, earth, and air; these elements interchange and turn into one another completely and combine to produce a universe animate, intelligent, spherical." (ibid., 341–343)

ϱ

One reason this passage is remarkable is that Alexander Polyhistor claims he found these tenets in the Pythagorean memoirs, and another is that Diogenes himself claims that Pythagoras wrote three books whereas historical research is unclear as to whether Pythagoras wrote any books at all. However, *my* major reason for wonder is that from my own long researches into Pythagoras, as well as ancient cultures, this account of Polyhistor is a brief, distilled, accurate version of Pythagoras' transcendental worldview! In fact, it is also an account of Plato's worldview as described—using secret and mythological symbolism—in the *Timaeus* dialogue.

I intend to use this template as a means by which to vindicate Pythagoras' worldview from all those who have criticized, marginalized, or dismissed him over the centuries. No longer need he remain in the shadows of history as an unknown, legendary figure, but for that very reason so much easier to attack when there was no exonerating evidence to prove his case.

It is my judgment that the template provided by Alexander Polyhistor is precisely the document to prove Pythagoras' case, and so crucial that one might repeat the words uttered by Guthrie: "A historian of science has claimed that Pythagoras' discovery changed the whole course of history" (Guthrie, HP, vol 1, 238).

The template mentioned is, on the one hand, the most succinct expression of any philosopher's worldview that I have ever encountered, and yet in its condensed and simplified form; it represents the most sophisticated understanding of the manifestation of the universe, one that is almost analogous to a Japanese *koan*. Let us see what Alexander Polyhistor has to say about the doctrines of Pythagoras, so they are made clear:

1) The principle of all things is the monad, or unit. In this statement Pythagoras uses the term monad, which I believe should be capitalized as Monad, for obvious reasons—Monad refers to God, as ultimate creator of the universe. Pythagoras also refers to the Monad as Unit, which is interpreted as One, namely the One containing everything in existence. The Monad, as God, is eternal, divine and changeless, and thus "exists" before, during, and after the universe is manifested in its eternal cosmic cycle.

2) Arising from this Monad the undefined dyad, or Two, serves as material substratum, which is cause.

Here Pythagoras makes several points. He tells us that the Monad, God, is the cause of everything. God creates the world. Then he tells us that from the Monad *arises* the undefined dyad, or Two. He explains that the undefined dyad is the material substratum, a term meaning that, via the Monad, God also creates and *exists as*, the material universe. The material substratum— namely the created world, or Nature, serves the Monad, or God. Thus, God, the Monad now has two forms—One is his original transcendental form, that which exists before creation, and Two is the world of Nature, the material substratum that exists simultaneously with the act of creation, or manifestation of the cosmos. By calling them a dyad Pythagoras communicates that these two principles, God and Nature, although seeming to be opposites, are in fact two different expressions of the same original principle, God. Within these few succinct lines, Pythagoras has also disclosed the world of number. There is nothing mysterious or opaque in it. As he clearly shows, God, the Monad is One, and the world of Nature, our universe, is Two.

3) From the Monad and the Undefined dyad spring numbers. This is interpreted, metaphysically, to mean that the *relation* between these two principles, bears fruit, in the number three.

(Oftentimes these three principles are said to be a divine triad—as is evidenced in many cultures of the world.)

4) From numbers, points (are manifested) A point is the first visible expression of number, meaning it can be plotted on a piece of paper. It is often determined to be dimensionless; therefore mirroring the transcendental, invisible Monad as source of the created universe.

5) From points, lines (are manifested). Stringing together a number of points in the end creates a line. A line is a one-dimensional figure (but conveys, for example) no depth.

6) From lines, planes (are manifested). Putting together three sides and making a triangle out of them creates an object—in space—but lacks solidity or material substance.

7) From plane figures, solid figures. Adding another line or two into a triangle, ends up creating a pyramid, a solid figure with length, depth, and breadth.

8) From solid figures, sensible bodies the elements of which are four: fire, water, earth and air. These elements interchange and turn into one another completely, and combine to produce a universe, animate, intelligent, spherical.

Here Pythagoras makes clear that all the things in the universe—rocks, insects, animals, birds, humans, and all of Nature (including the Moon, Sun and stars), have contained in them, in one way or another, the four elements. It is the endless permutations of these four interchangeable elements that combine to produce a universe, which is alive, intelligent, and spherical by design.

What one notes is that this is a blueprint for the manifestation of the entire universe, a process that takes literally eons of time to accomplish. And what it communicates is that at each descending level, the energy of the Monad, operating through the indefinite dyad, manifests itself more and more deeply into density until it finally arrives at the natural elements that combine in a multitude of ways to produce our material universe.

This brief explanation of Pythagoras' worldview is useful in two ways. First, to my knowledge, it is the first time that a document revealing the true, transcendental doctrines of Pythagoras has been presented to the public, and for this we owe Alexander Polyhistor—and Diogenes Laertius—debts of immense gratitude! Second, it is a template against which one can discuss and judge Philolaus' interpretation of Pythagoras' doctrines.

CHAPTER 2

PYTHAGORAS AND SCIENCE

It should come as no surprise to a serious reader that for an account of Pythagoras' cosmology we must depend upon scientists and mathematicians rather than philosophers, ancient or modern. They give a more factual interpretation. That is why the accounts of Sir Thomas Heath, in his book *Aristarchus of Samos: The Ancient Copernican,* and J. L. E. Dreyer in his book *A History of Astronomy from Thales to Kepler,* are so invaluable for our knowledge of Pythagoras. And, let us be clear, grateful as we are to Heath and Dreyer, they are reporting the scientific facts, and make no pretence of knowing about or reporting on the metaphysical and/or mystical aspects of Pythagoras' worldview. But, they contrast the views of the early Presocratics with those of Pythagoras.

The full account of Pythagoras' science and mathematics can be found in Heath and he begins by saying: "Pythagoras, undoubtedly one of the greatest names in the history of science, whose interests were as varied as those of Thales, but with the difference that, whereas Thales' knowledge was mostly of practical application, with Pythagoras the subjects of which he treats become sciences for the first time" (Heath, AOS, 45). That is the first remarkable statement made about Pythagoras.

Heath continues, "Mathematicians know him, of course, mostly or exclusively, as the reputed discoverer of the theorem of Euclid" (I 47), the Pythagorean theorem; however, whereas his share in the discovery of this proposition is much disputed, there is no doubt that he was the first to make theoretical geometry a subject forming part of a liberal education, and to investigate its first principles.

With him, too, began the Theory of Numbers.

A mathematician then of brilliant achievements, he was also the inventor of the science of acoustics, an astronomer of great originality, a theologian and moral reformer, founder of a brotherhood which admits comparison with the order of mediaeval chivalry.

The epoch-making discovery that musical tones depend on numerical proportions, the octave representing the proportion of 2:1; the fifth 3:2; and the fourth 4:3, may with sufficient certainty be attributed to Pythagoras himself; as may the first exposition of the theory of *means,* and of proportions in general applied to commensurable quantities—i.e., those quantities the ratio between which can be expressed as a ratio between whole numbers. The all-pervading character of number being thus shown, what wonder that the Pythagoreans came to declare that number is the essence of all things? The connection so discovered between number and music would also lead not unnaturally to the idea of the harmony of the heavenly bodies" (Heath, AOS, 46–47).

Heath then mentions that Philolaus, born one hundred years after Pythagoras, was the first to "write an exposition of the Pythagorean system." Heath adds that due to this fact it is hard to separate out which accomplishments may be attributed to Pythagoras himself and which may be attributed to Philolaus. Heath refers to Aristotle as having this difficulty, and says that the "account which he (Aristotle) gives of the Pythagorean planetary system corresponds to the system of Philolaus as we know it from the Doxographi."

Remarkably, Heath concludes: *"For Pythagoras' own system, therefore, that of Philolaus affords no guide*; we have to seek for traces in the other writers of the end of the sixth and beginning of the fifth centuries, of opinions borrowed from him or polemics directed against him (Tannery, op. cit., 203). On these principles we have seen reason to believe that he [Pythagoras] was the first to maintain that the Earth is spherical, and on the basis of that assumption, to distinguish the five zones" (ibid., 48). Heath says it is uncertain how Pythagoras came to conclude that the Earth was spherical, but states, "Whatever may have been the ground, the declaration that the Earth was spherical was a great step toward the true, the Copernican view of the universe" (ibid., 48–49).

Heath adds, "It may well be [though we are not told] that Pythagoras, for the same reason, gave the same spherical shape to the Sun and Moon and even the stars, in which case the way lay open for the discovery of the true cause of eclipses and phases of the Moon." There is no doubt that Pythagoras' own system was geocentric. (As will be shown later, Aristotle, although baffled, recorded that he believed the Pythagoreans subscribed to a heliocentric system.) We are also told directly that Pythagoras regarded the universe as living, intelligent, spherical, enclosing the Earth in the middle, the Earth, too, being spherical in shape. Further it seems clear that he held that the universe rotated about an axis passing through the center of the Earth. Thus, we are told by Aristotle, "Some [of the Pythagoreans] say that *time* is the motion of the whole [universe]; others that it is the sphere itself" (*Phys.*, iv. 10, 218 a 33) and by Aetius that "Pythagoras held *time* to be the sphere of the enveloping (heaven)" (Diels, 318). I underscore the fact that Pythagoras was the first to include time as an "originating principle." There is no mention of such a hypothesis in the Presocratics.

Heath then says, "Alcmaeon and the mathematicians hold that the planets have a motion from west to east, in a direction opposite to that of the fixed stars" (ibid., 345). "This passage is also the first we hear of the important distinction between the diurnal revolution of the fixed stars from east to west and the independent movement of the planets *in the opposite direction*," says Heath. He adds, "The Ionians say nothing of it." He wonders whether Anaximenes had also discovered it and says, "Anaxagoras and Democritus rejected it; the discovery, therefore, appears to belong to the Pythagorean school, and in view of its character it is much more likely to have been made by the Master himself than by the physician of Croton." The rest of Alcmaeon's astronomy is on a much lower level. Heath concludes by saying, "We have also the evidence of Theon of Smyrna, who states categorically that Pythagoras was the first to notice that the planets move in independent circles" (Heath, AOS, 50).

Heath's conclusions about Pythagoras' cosmology are as follows: "It appears probable, therefore, that the theory of Pythagoras himself was that the universe, the Earth, and the other heavenly bodies are spherical in shape, that the Earth rests in the center, that the sphere of the fixed stars has a daily rotation from east to west about an axis passing through the center of the Earth, and that the planets have an independent movement of their own in a sense opposite to that of the daily rotation, i.e., from west to east."

Here, I would make six important points:

1) Heath does not appear to have been aware, or accepted any statement as to how Pythagoras conceived the origin of our universe. The template from Alexander Polyhistor has already indicated that the Monad, or God, created the universe.

2) It is a remarkable declaration by Heath that although Aristotle maintains that the Pythagorean planetary system corresponds to that of Philolaus, he, Heath believes this system of Philolaus "affords no guide" to that of Pythagoras (ibid., 38).

3) It is also important that, contrary to a host of others, Heath prefers to go back and "seek traces in the other writers of the end of the sixth and the beginning of the fifth century B.C. in order to discover Pythagoras' own system" (ibid., 48).

This statement has great relevance because, as we know, most academics and historians in the Western tradition have cavalierly lumped together all early references in the doxography relating to the sixth or fifth centuries BC as one "homogenous group." And a scholar such as Burkert—though he is not the only one—wants to move all views surrounding Pythagoras in the sixth or early fifth century BC to Plato's time and then mirror Plato's ideas and those of his students back to the time of Pythagoras, as if they were Platonic in origin. As a scientist and mathematician Heath is more interested in those early hypotheses that derived from a time as close as possible to the actual lifetime of Pythagoras, whereas many modern academics prefer to rely on statements and theories far removed from that time. Heath's view will hopefully inspire research and debate on the importance of this early time period.

4) Heath states that Pythagoras' own system was geocentric. This is not surprising despite the fact that rumors of a possible heliocentric view were stated by Aristotle of the Pythagoreans,

and of course the actual displacement of Earth at the center of the cosmos in favor of the central fire by Philolaus. But, as the great genius, Sir Isaac Newton tells us, philosophers (such as Pythagoras) were so concerned with ridicule that they "hid the truth" of their theories from the general public.... In the case of Pythagoras, the heliocentric theory depended on research, experiments, and proofs from his work on the numerical relationships discovered in the musical scale (octave 2:1; fifth 3:2; fourth 4:3), and he eventually posited consonant numerical relationships obtained between the planets in our solar system. One can appreciate Pythagoras' concern with ridicule about theories that were centuries, if not two thousand years ahead of his time! In fact, as Godwin tells us, Pythagoras, beneath parables of this sort (i.e., that his researches *appeared* tied to the Earth as center of the cosmos) was hiding his own system and the true harmony of the heavens—i.e., the heliocentric theory.... Newton it is said, was aware that "Pythagoras numbered his musical tones from the Earth...but *he taught* that...the weights of the planets toward the Sun (emphasis added) were reciprocally as the squares of their distances from the Sun.".... It is understandable that Heath believed Pythagoras had a geocentric system when that is what Pythagoras wished the general public of his time to believe. However, Newton's affirmation of Pythagoras as the one who discovered the heliocentric theory in the sixth century BC is crucial, and will be discussed in the chapters on the Harmony of the Spheres and the Heliocentric Theory. (Godwin, 305–307)

5) As for Aristotle, though baffled, he had recorded the rumor that the Pythagoreans subscribed to a *heliocentric* system. In that case, it would no longer be true that the universe "enclosed the Earth in the middle." However, it seems likely that Heath had inadvertently followed Aristotle's planetary system, because it displaced the central fire of Philolaus and put the Earth back at the center of our cosmos.

6) None of the Presocratics referred to time as an indispensable component of our cosmos, but Pythagoras shows that the

movements of the Sun, Moon, planets, and fixed stars are all *governed* by time.

We can conclude that the heliocentric theory of Pythagoras was the crowning cosmological achievement of an acclaimed and brilliant mathematician, scientist, and astronomer who, it is stated, in the main, introduced these ideas into Greece. Thus, there is no question in my mind that Pythagoras himself discovered the heliocentric theory, and that some people in the ancient world, including Aristotle, heard veiled rumors about it, which they repeated in print.

As for Dreyer, we would do well to recall that, for him the Ionian school had not advanced very far in the direction of a rational idea of the universe. "The Earth was flat, the fixed stars were attached to a vault, the planets are barely mentioned, and the nature of the Sun and Moon imperfectly understood" (Dreyer, 17). He introduces us to the school of Pythagoras in the following terms: "It is time that we should turn our attention to a most important school in which mathematics and astronomy were assiduously cultivated and which exercised a powerful influence on the advance of knowledge" (ibid., 34).

One important point raised by Dreyer relates to the motion of the fixed stars. Dreyer comments: "To the modern reader this suggests a knowledge of the precession of the equinoxes, as this shows itself as a very slow motion of the stars from west to east... There seems indeed no reason to believe that any Greek astronomer before Hipparchus had the slightest knowledge of precession" (Dreyer, 48). Here, again, it is understandable that due to what he knew at the time, he could not be persuaded to believe that precession was known in the sixth century BC. However, modern research has proved—especially as shown in *The Dawning of Astronomy,* the remarkable book by J. Norman Lockyer, by precise scientific investigation of the orientation of ancient Egyptian temples—that the Egyptians were fully aware of and incorporated in a most sophisticated fashion, the laws of precession (among other things) into the building of *very* ancient sacred temples.

Dreyer's account of the Pythagoreans is somewhat more complicated, even dismissive, than Heath's, but he concludes by saying, "It is impossible to review this strange system of the world without a certain feeling of admiration. The boldness of conception which inspired the Pythagoreans with the idea that the Earth need not necessarily be the principal body, at rest in the center of the universe, contrasts in a remarkable manner with the prevailing ideas, not only of their own time, but of the next two thousand years" (Dreyer, 49).

CHAPTER 3

PHILOLAUS: AN OVERVIEW

Commentators—ancient and modern—tell us that Philolaus (ca. 470–390 BC) was a student of Pythagoras, and since Pythagoras was born around 572 BC, the length of time between their births was approximately a hundred years. Aristotle is considered the first to give an account of the works of Philolaus and the Pythagoreans. He was born around 310 BC—one hundred and sixty years after Philolaus, and two hundred and sixty years after Pythagoras.

Western philosophers and historians have followed mainly the formidable reputation of Aristotle in their discussions and acceptance of what I like to call the "Philolaic philosophy." However if we turn back to Charles H. Kahn, *Pythagoras and the Pythagoreans: A Brief History*, we note a great deal of controversy among Western academics as to the author of the discoveries of Pythagoras, or "the so-called Pythagoreans," as Aristotle liked to describe them. For example, Erik Frank claimed that all such discoveries were really "the achievement of certain Italian mathematicians of Plato's time." Walter Burkert claimed that all of Pythagoras' theories hearkened back to Plato's time, and were reflected back upon Pythagoras, making it *appear* that they originated from a Pre-Platonic time. And Kahn himself tells us that since Pythagoras left no written records, "the history of Pythagorean philosophy must begin with the first known Pythagorean book, *On Nature*. This is the work of Philolaus in the last half of the fifth century BC" (Kahn, 25).

Kahn reminds us that the fragments of Philolaus (discussed in Carl Huffman's scholarly work, *Philolaus of Croton: Pythagorean and Presocratic*) "reflect essentially the same worldview that is attributed to the Pythagoreans by Aristotle and ascribed to Philolaus and the Pythagoreans in the later doxography deriving from Theophrastus. So it will be convenient to refer to this, the oldest attested version of Pythagorean theory, as the system of Philolaus, without prejudging the question of its originality" (ibid., 23).

There are several reasons why Philolaus is so pivotal in Pythagorean thought: 1) crucial discoveries of cosmology and astronomy are attributed to him; 2) he is famous in the history books as the originator of the most remarkable—and controversial—view, reported by Aristotle himself, namely the "heliocentric" view that displaced the Earth from the center of our cosmos and designated it as merely another planet orbiting the center! As we know, science tells us that the heliocentric theory was not discovered until the sixteenth century AD by Nicholas Copernicus—nearly two thousand years after the time of Philolaus. Galileo affirmed the heliocentric theory, and Kepler mentions Philolaus as one among other ancients who had explored the displacement of the Earth and as a starting point for his own astronomical discoveries. Nevertheless, let us not get ahead of ourselves. What do commentators—ancient and modern—tell us about Philolaus?

Although popularly described as a pupil of Pythagoras, he is designated by Huffman as a Pythagorean and Presocratic, and is acclaimed for writing (at least) one book. In that work his main philosophical, cosmological and astronomical statements are made public. As such, a brief overview of his principles is in order. We shall set aside the controversial question as to whether Philolaus wrote one book, with the title, *On Nature*, or whether Plato "wrote Dion in Sicily to buy three Pythagorean books from Philolaus for 100 minae" (Huffman, 13).

As Huffman tells us, Philolaus' book *On Nature* begins with a statement of his central thesis, under the heading "Basic Principles":

Fragment 1: "Nature in the world order was fitted together both out of things which are unlimited and out of things which are limiting, both the world order as a whole and everything in it" (ibid., 37).

He adds, also under the heading "Basic Principles":

Fragment 6: "Concerning nature and harmony the situation is this: the being of things, which is eternal, and nature in itself admit of divine and not human knowledge, except that it was impossible for any of the things that are and are known by us to have come to be, if the being of the things from which the world-order came together, both the limiting things and the unlimited things, did not preexist." (ibid.)

Apart from the possibility of the preexistence of "things" the question remains: Exactly *how* are the limiting and unlimited things fitted together? Huffman explains that it is due to what is described as a harmonia, and it is somewhat surprising that the fragment *referring* to the harmonia is a continuation of fragment 6 in Basic Principles. It reads:

But since these beginnings pre-existed and were neither alike nor even related it would have been impossible for them to be ordered if a harmony had not come upon them, in whatever way it came to be.... Like things and related things did not in addition require any harmony, but things that are unlike and not even related nor of [the same speed?], it is necessary that such things be bonded together by harmony, if they are going to be held in an order

The text of the fragment continues as fragment 6a. The words used in these fragments—*world order* and *harmony*—imply mathematics, and Huffman deals with the question of what role numbers and mathematics play in the system of Philolaus.

Fragment 4: "And indeed, all the things that are known have number. For it is not possible that anything whatsoever be understood or known without this."

Regarding cosmology, Huffman explains, "The primary sources for Philolaus' cosmology are seemingly very meager indeed (fragments 7 and 17)—about six lines in total, but they are absolutely crucial for understanding Philolaus' philosophy and for evaluating Aristotle's accounts of Pythagoreanism." He deals first with fragment 17 (from the Bacchae of Philolaus):

The world order is one. It began to come to be right up at the middle, and from the middle [came to be] upward in the same way as downward, and the things in the middle are symmetrical with those below. For, in the lower [regions] the lowest part [for the upper regions] like the highest and similarly for the rest. For both [the higher and lower] have the same relationship to the middle, except that their positions are reversed. (Huffman, 215)

Interestingly, fragment 7, the only other cosmological fragment, appears in the appendix subtitled "Above and Below, left and right in Aristotle's reports on the Pythagoreans." Because it is so brief, Huffman calls upon Aristotle to preface the fragment by stating: "The world is one, and from the unlimited, time and breath were brought in, as well as the void which distinguishes the place of each thing in each case." Huffman discusses this issue (215–216), and eventually, on page 226 discloses:

Fragment 7: "The first thing fitted together, the one in the center of the sphere, is called the hearth."

One cannot help but notice that in the Philolaus fragment there are no references to time, breath, or the void—as are found in the Aristotle preface. And, let us further note, that these two fragments constitute the entire exposition of Philolaus' cosmology! As far as Astronomy is concerned, Huffman states the following: "The only fragments which are relevant to the astronomical system are fragments 7 and 17, which I have already discussed in relation to Philolaus' cosmogony" (Huffman, 242–243).

In other words—there are no genuine fragments from Philolaus on the crucial topic of Astronomy, subtitled in Huffman's book as: "Texts *relevant* to the astronomical system of Philolaus (including Testimonia A16, A17, and A21)."

The names included under this chapter are Aristotle and various doxographers. In fact, as Huffman tells us, after Aristotle "the second source for early Pythagorean astronomy is the doxographical tradition represented by Aetius, which ultimately goes back to Aristotle's pupil—Theophrastus (texts 7–9). Here we find the same astronomical system mentioned in Aristotle, but this time it is ascribed to Philolaus" (Huffman, p. 242).

This, in a nutshell, is Philolaus' philosophy: The world is fitted together from limiting and unlimited things by means of a harmonia, itself based upon number relationships. And the philosophy is controversial owing to the doctrine that the Earth is displaced from the center of the cosmos and is replaced by the central fire, called the hearth, which is said to be the first thing fitted together.

It is a brief overview, but each topic will be investigated fully in the chapters that follow, beginning with "Limiters and Unlimiteds."

CHAPTER 4

LIMITERS AND UNLIMITEDS

Huffman begins by explaining that Philolaus did not tell us what he *meant* by *limiters* and *unlimited;* nor did he provide a *single example* of them in the fragments (Huffman, 37). There are various hypotheses (i.e., Burkert, Schofield, Barnes) based on the fragments, but in the case of Aristotle, his account is based upon the Pythagoreans. For Huffman this would mean Philolaus, because he first published a book considered to be by a "Pythagorean." For Aristotle limiters and unlimiteds are assigned a secondary role to the real star of Pythagorean metaphysics, namely number. On this view limiters and unlimiteds become singular instead of plural and come to assume the principles of *Limit* and *Unlimited,* and owing to the influence of Plato and Aristotle, according to Huffman, these terms become totally detached from the phenomenal world (ibid., 38).

Huffman challenges the interpretation of Aristotle, saying that for Philolaus it is the limiters and unlimiteds that are primary, not number; they are plural, not singular, and they arise from Nature. Huffman traces Philolaus' doctrines to Presocratic sources, especially Parmenides and Anaxagoras. For Philolaus, limiters and unlimiteds are "not treated as abstract principles divorced from the world, but rather as manifest features of the world" (ibid., 40).

Huffman points out that in fact limiters and unlimiteds do not by themselves explain the world order and thus a third principle, the harmonia "supervenes" in order to bind limiters and unlimiteds into a world order. Huffman adds: *if we* could find explicit examples of things that are "fitted together" we ought to be able to identify "what is limiting and what is unlimited in such a compound" (ibid., 41). Huffman posits that such an example is to be found in the next fragment:

Fragment 7: "The first thing fitted together, the one in the center of the sphere is called the hearth."

Here Huffman equates the hearth with the "central fire"; the central fire as the unlimited, and the middle of the sphere as a limiter because it determines the fire's position spatially. (We notice that Huffman here does not deal with the *origin* of the sphere in this equation.)

But Huffman does refer to the sphere in fragment 17, in which he admits there is no reference to limiters and unlimiteds, nor any reference to "fitting together."

Fragment 17: "The world order is one; it began to come to be right up at the middle and from the middle [came to be] upward in the same way as downward [etc.]" (ibid., 42).

Huffman says the notion of development in all directions equally, which "is inherent in the spherical shape" is one of the important limiters that is combined with a variety of unlimiteds in order to generate the actual cosmic order (ibid., 43). To provide more examples of unlimiteds, Huffman relies on Aristotle, (whom he suggests derived his views from Philolaus):

Fragment 201: "The universe is one, and it drew from the unlimited time, breath, and void, which in each case distinguishes the place of each thing" (ibid.).

After a brief discussion focusing on how to contextualize breath, void and time—namely: Are they drawn from outside the cosmos, or are they defined as unlimiteds? Huffman, remarkably, states, "This passage of Aristotle is as close as we get to a series of examples of what Philolaus meant by *unlimiteds*" (ibid., 44). Huffman seems to have forgotten that Philolaus had never specified what he meant by limiters and unlimiteds, nor had he ever given examples of them. Huffman has also omitted to mention that Aristotle derives time, breath, and void *from* the unlimited, not that they should be construed *as* unlimiteds. However, Huffman pushes onward with his exposition. He states that time, breath, and void must each be seen as a continuum, "where none of them is defined by any set quantity or boundaries" (ibid., 43). He adds that Aristotle made a *careless formulation* when he defined void as that which distinguishes the "place" of each thing, whereas Philolaus would have seen the void as that in which limits are set. Huffman concludes: "Thus we now have a list of *four unlimiteds* (fire, breath, time, and void) which Philolaus saw as having a role in cosmogony" (ibid., 44).

Huffman claims, "Fr 6a presents another helpful example of what Philolaus may have meant by a fitting together of limiters and unlimiteds" (ibid., 44). Huffman says, after arguing in fragment 6 for the necessity of a harmonia, or "fitting together" to hold limiters and unlimiteds together, in fragment 6a Philolaus goes on to specify the "*size* of the fitting together" and "what follows is an account of the structure of the 'Pythagorean' diatonic scale, or attunement, that is identical to the scale that is presupposed in the *Timaeus*" (ibid.).

Under the heading "Authenticity" for fragment 6a, Huffman notes that the later tradition of Xenocrates attributed music theory to Pythagoras himself (ibid., 147). From this information Huffman suggests it is quite plausible to see the undefined continuum of possible musical pitches as the unlimited. On the other hand the limiters would be the boundaries we establish in this continuum by picking out specific pitches. The example Huffman gives is that of a monochord— whose strings and indefinite number of pitches could be compared to the unlimited whereas stops placed along it, which determine specific pitches, would be defined as limiters.

Huffman claims the example shows that limiters and unlimiteds alone will not produce an ordered system; "not just any set of pitches will produce a musically ordered set: such a set *only results* when the unlimited continuum is limited in accordance with a *harmonia* which determines a *pleasing* set of limits in the unlimited in accordance with number" (ibid., 45). At the same time, Huffman also cautions us that Philolaus never equated number or harmony with limit.

Huffman tells us that words like Nature, world order, and harmonia "have had a long history in Presocratic thought" (ibid., 49), pointing out that the "concept of the unlimited has played a central role, and that Parmenides has something to say about limit. And yet he states that Philolaus is not arguing for limiters and unlimiteds in the way of the Presocratic tradition, but sees them as manifest features of

the world and that therefore both must be recognized as basic components of it, since one cannot be derived from the other" (ibid., 49).
Huffman looks to the Presocratic tradition to find possible sources for
the above terms. In respect to the term unlimited, he refers back to
Anaximander as positing that it was "the starting point from which
the cosmos arose—namely a limitless expanse of indeterminate nature
out of which emerge the basic elements which constitute our world"
(ibid., 50). He also states that Anaximander emphasized opposites,
such as hot and cold, dry and wet, and the world as emerging in part
out of the "balanced conflict" of these opposites. Anaximenes, a pupil
of Anaximander, hypothesized the "basic stuff" as air. And Anaxagoras includes a list of unlimiteds—such as "air, aither (fr. 1), dry, wet,
hot, cold, bright, dark (fr. 4), dense, and rare (fr. 12)" (ibid., 50). Parmenides had argued that the unlimited had to be held in the bonds
of limit in order for it to be intelligible" (ibid.). Melissus applied the
term unlimited to his one being but argued that "there could only be
one such unlimited," whereas Philolaus assumes that the world has "to
arise from origins that are plural" (ibid.).

In conclusion, Huffman states that, for Philolaus, the unlimited and
the limited (as basic principles) "must be invoked in order to explain
reality" (ibid.). However, Huffman suggests that "Philolaus goes further by stating that these basic principles are a natural development
from earlier Presocratic thought, differing from the list of Anaxagoras,
"in that they are not determined by any quantity, such as water, air, fire,
but rather simply mark a continuum of possible quantities" (ibid., 51)

Huffman holds that Philolaus has introduced "recognition of a
distinct class of unlimiteds" (namely time, void, and musical pitch),
which is probably and indirectly based upon the introduction of limiters, along with the unlimiteds as "basic constituents of reality" (ibid.).
He suggests that whereas prior Presocratics had hypothesized quantities such as fire, air, or water as the origins of our world, Huffman's
list of unlimited—time, void, and musical pitch—(all of which *are*
non-material) actually constitutes part of the structure and order of
our world.

Finally, Huffman wants to make clear that in dealing with unlimited and limiters Philolaus is "approaching something like a distinction

between form and matter, but his thinking is still very much in the Presocratic mode" (ibid.), a point Huffman underscores by noting that Aristotle criticized the Pythagoreans as "developing principles for a different sort of reality, (but) talk about nothing but the sensible world" (ibid., 52), and that Plato in the *Philebus* presents the notion of unlimiteds and limiters "as something handed down from his forefathers who lived closer to the gods" (ibid.).

Huffman concludes "Thus, Philolaus' adoption of limiters and unlimiteds as principles makes sense as a development of Presocratic ideas which anticipates Aristotelian and Platonic distinctions in interesting ways but not that between the intelligible and the sensible, which become important later" (ibid., 53).

COMMENTARY

The first thing to note about Huffman's exposition of Philolaus' limiters and unlimiteds (ibid., 88) is that of a disagreement between Aristotle and Philolaus. Huffman bemoans the fact that Aristotle says the "real star" of Pythagorean metaphysics is number, and replies that for Philolaus it is limiters and unlimiteds, not number, that is primary.

Perhaps this conflict is not unsurprising since Huffman tells us that Philolaus' doctrines have Presocratic sources, especially Parmenides and Anaxagoras, whereas Aristotle is attempting to understand Pythagorean mathematics. As we know (*Meta I*, 5 986a 17), Aristotle equated unlimited with even and limited with odd, and despite the possible influence of Philolaus, disagreed with Philolaus' Presocratic conclusion that limiters and unlimiteds are primary, not Pythagorean numbers. There are other instances when Aristotle disagrees with Philolaus on philosophical points, and, as a result, we must wonder whether Aristotle had misgivings about some of Philolaus' other pronouncements.

For example, Philolaus had mentioned the third term, the harmonia that would "supervene" to bind limiters and unlimiteds into a world order. It was Huffman, not Philolaus, who added that if explicit examples could be found of things that were "fitted together" we "ought to be able to identify what is limiting and what is unlimited in such a compound" (Huffman, 41). Huffman offers an example:

Fragment 7: "The first thing fitted together, the one in the center of the sphere is called 'the hearth.'"

One may speculate that Aristotle, with his towering intellect and gift for scientific classification, would question the above declaration on the very grounds that it hearkened back to fanciful and inadequate pronouncements about reality voiced by other Presocratics. For Aristotle the scientist things were not "fitted together," nor was there a hearth at the center of the cosmos. Here we have another major disagreement between Aristotle and Philolaus.

Nonetheless, the real conflict lies between the interpretation of originating cosmic principles by Philolaus and by Pythagoras. First, as I have shown, Pythagoras' doctrine of originating principles begins with the transcendental Monad, God, which is eternal, invisible, unchanging, and divine. For Pythagoras the material world is a projection, an emanation of the Monad into the undefined dyad, the material substratum that constitutes the entire cosmos, and from thence, through numbers and ever-denser dimensions and densifications, comes into full physical manifestation as the material world.

There is no possibility that things are "fitted together" for Pythagoras because there is an internal logic and outflowing mathematical structure to the universe that is harmonious in its origin. Also we may note that the great mathematician Heath has confirmed that Pythagoras was the first to posit the universe as a sphere. Therefore the sphere Philolaus mentions is not an original discovery, but something learned directly or indirectly from other Pythagoreans who probably lived later than Pythagoras himself.

As far as the statement "the first thing fitted together, the one in the center of the sphere is called the hearth" is concerned, Pythagoras would have placed it in the category of fanciful statements attributed to the Presocratics, because the term "hearth" is not based upon scientific observations nor on mathematical principles or conclusions regarding the universe. (We will explore this topic further in the chapter on astronomy.) Huffman then refers to Philolaus' fragment 17. He admits there is no reference to limiters and unlimiteds, nor to "fitting together," but quotes Philolaus:

Fragment 17 "The world order is one" (ibid., 42)

—which is in direct contradiction to Philoaus' declaration that limiters and unlimited are multiple; they are material, they arise from Nature and they need a third term, a harmonia to fit them together. Needless to say, Philolaus cannot have it both ways.

To provide more examples of unlimiteds, Huffman, not Philolaus, calls upon Aristotle (fr. 201) for assistance. His quotation is as follows: "The universe is one, and it drew from the unlimited, time, breath, and void, which in each case distinguishes the place of each thing." Here Aristotle pronounces that the universe is one, and that from the unlimited (singular) the universe drew time, breath, and void. We must note that Philolaus himself makes no mention of time, breath, or void in his work. What is novel is that Huffman claims time, breath, and void are each to be defined as a continuum. But whereas Aristotle is telling us that from the unlimited, the universe drew time, breath, and void, *as limiters,* Huffman concludes that the passage of Aristotle is as close as we get to a series of examples of what Philolaus meant by unlimiteds.

Aside from the fact that Huffman had told us that Philolaus himself never said what he meant by unlimiteds or limiters, nor had he given an example of them, Huffman seems to have determined that time, breath, and void are to be defined as unlimiteds. There is no evidence that Aristotle defined them as unlimiteds; in fact the opposite appears to be the case because Aristotle clearly stated he was referring to the unlimited as their source. A deeper contemplation of the Aristotelian statement is therefore required.

TIME, VOID, AND BREATH

Aristotle declared that the universe drew from the unlimited, time, void, and breath. There are others, even Plato, who questioned whether the eternal realm was beyond the boundary of our universe, or not. There are endless speculations about the apeiron, and whether it was a translucent "material" having origin in our universe, and of course the ancients pondered the mysterious assumption that the universe "breathes." All that is indeed speculation. However, we only have to look back at the ancient scriptures to discover a forgotten truth, lost because so many of the leading scientists and modern philosophers have a material worldview.

What is found in ancient Hinduism and ancient Buddhism, as well as Christianity, is that the world has a *transcendental* origin, a divine origin. Pythagoras refers to this principle, what Christians call God, as the Monad—the Monad that represents the One universe, the One that is absolute, indestructible, eternal, the One that contains all things within it as a Unity. The Christian Bible also refers to a time *before* God manifested this universe. The first verse of the Gospel according to St. John in The New Testament declares, "In the beginning was the Word, and the Word was *with* God, and the Word *was* God." Although many may interpret that sentence as referring to Jesus, the Christ made flesh, it can equally mean that God exists in his Word *before* the universe is manifested in its material form. For Pythagoras, the word he used for this divine principle is *Monad,* perhaps signifying that it now required a Western flavor, a scientific cast, one that implies numbers and mathematics.

When, therefore Aristotle refers to time, void, and breath, he is inferring that they are limiters. Is he in the Philolaus tradition when he makes that declaration? Or is he adhering to his own conclusions? The answer is unclear because Huffman seems to arbitrarily change Aristotle's limiteds into Philolaus' unlimiteds. However, the view of the ancient scriptures regarding time, void, and breath has its origin in a very ancient teaching. I will give the Hindu version, but it will be found in the other ancient scriptures of the East as well. The Hindu version states that the universe is eternal; it has no beginning and it has no end. In the cosmic period before it manifests the material universe, it is wrapped up in its own eternality. In the Hindu version, this period of apparent rest is called *pralaya,* the "time" when the universe rests within its own divine Source. But, according to its own cosmic law, the divine source, the Monad, God, manifests the world we know, the world of time and space and materiality. In the Indian system this is referred to as the "outbreath"—the divine Source is seen to *breathe out the entire universe in one primordial expression of expansion and joy*. Perhaps *this* is the source of the speculation about whether, and how the universe "breathes."

And, as Pythagoras has demonstrated, the Absolute, or God, first *breathes out* the undefined dyad—that part of Himself which is also divine and eternal, but which "limits" part of itself to take on the cloak of materiality. And at that cosmic "moment," when the divine Source breathes out the entire universe, the duality of time and space is born (or as Aristotle calls it, *time, breath,* and *void*). And, spontaneously with that original "split" the series of dualities is manifested: light–dark, male–female, left–right, up–down, good–bad, etc. These are the principles that govern the material world. This is why Plato says, in a moment of inspiration, that our world is a copy of the eternal one and that as a result "time is the moving image of eternity."

And at the conclusion of the cosmic cycle, a cycle encompassing untold eons of "time" the material universe withdraws back into its eternal source. To give a parallel that makes it understandable, it would be as if you woke up one morning after a long sleep; you engaged in all the activities of your day; and at the end, at night, you enter again the world of sleep. The next "day" you repeat this cycle. It is no coincidence, of course, that when you are born into this earthly world, it is characterized by the fact that you take your first breath. Our breath is the first sign of materiality of birth, and it is the last vestige of materiality before we pass back into eternity. It is a repeatable cycle, tied in our world, to a cycle of day and night spanning twenty-four hours. In the case of the cosmos, as said, the cycle encompasses eons of time.

If we wish to emulate Pythagoras and Plato when we approach the question of the origin of our world, we must not blindly accept the endless speculations of scientists and philosophers who are still trying to defend the theory that our universe is material in origin. If you recall the quotation by Alexander Polyhistor (19–20) you will see that the universe goes through at least nine or ten levels of descent before it finally arrives at the material elements—those very elements that the Presocratics insist are the origin of the cosmos. The levels of descent are listed, in order:

Monad
Undefined dyad
Numbers
Points
Lines
Plane figures
Solid figures
Sensible bodies
The four elements: fire, water, earth, and air.

As mentioned, all of the dualities—light–dark, male–female, left–right, good–bad, and so on—are also spontaneously manifested in the "moment" of cosmic rebirth. One cannot help noting that Pythagoras' doctrine of cosmic manifestation bears no comparison to Philolaus' Presocratic attempt to seek for the origins of our universe in quasi-elements such as the "central" fire, limiters and unlimiteds.

PLATO'S PHILEBUS

Most Western scholars cannot resist dragging Plato into the question of limiters and unlimiteds, although the single reference found in the *Philebus,* a later dialogue, focuses on the topic as to whether wisdom or pleasure is the greater good. Interestingly Socrates tells Protarchus that when he was asked what the good was he had suggested intelligence, knowledge, mind, and so on as being good. But then Socrates adds, "Knowledge taken in its entirety will seem to be a plurality in which this knowledge is unlike that" (*Philebus,* 14, a–c).

Plato finds the same situation regarding pleasure, for he writes, "Of course the mere word 'pleasure' suggests a unity, but surely the forms it assumes are of all sorts and, in a sense, unlike each other" (ibid., 12-c).

Socrates suggests that each of the above cases reduces to an argument of the One vs. the many—a mystery permeating ancient Greek philosophy. He asks, "To begin with [is there] a single unity [i.e., of wisdom or of pleasure], but which subsequently comes to be in the infinite number of things that come into being—an identical unity being thus found simultaneously in unity and in plurality. Is it torn in pieces or does the whole of it...get apart from itself?" (ibid., 15-b).

Socrates concludes, "We get this identity of the one and the many cropping up everywhere as a result of the sentences we utter" (ibid., 14-d, Hamilton and Cairns).

Protarchus urges Socrates to find a way to solve this "bothersome business" and Socrates replies to him that he has a method that he has used, one to which he has always been devoted; it is a method easy to indicate but difficult to employ. It is "the instrument through which every discovery ever made in the sphere of the arts and sciences has been brought to light" (ibid., 16 b-c).

Socrates then goes on to utter the words that many Western scientific scholars have latched onto regarding Plato's position re: limiters and unlimiteds:

There is a gift of the gods...which they let fall from their abode, and it was through Prometheus, or one like him, that it reached humankind, *together with a fire exceeding bright.* The men of old who were better than ourselves and dwelt nearer the gods, passed on this gift in the form of a saying. All things, so it ran, that are ever said to be, consist of *a one and a many,* and have in their nature a *conjunction of limit and unlimitedness.* This then being the ordering of things we ought, they said, whatever it be that we are dealing with, to assume a single form and search for it, for we shall find it there contained; then if we have laid hold of that, we must go on from one form to look for two, if the case admits of there being two; otherwise for three or some other number of forms. And we must do the same again with each of the 'ones' thus reached, until we come to see not merely that the one we started with is a one and an unlimited many, but also just how many it is. But we are not to apply the character of unlimitedness to our plurality until we have discerned the total number of forms the thing in question has intermediate between its *one and its unlimited number.* It is only then, when we have done that, that we may let each one of all these intermediate forms pass away into the unlimited and cease bothering about them. There, then, that is how the gods, as I told you, have committed us to the task of inquiry, of learning, and of teaching one another. (*Philebus,* 16-d-e)

Two things may be remarked on here. First, Socrates says the guidance from the gods was to first look for a single form and discover the many in the multitude of its expressions—a classic technique used by Socrates in all the dialogues up to the *Republic*. The mere reference to limiters and unlimitedness here in Plato is clearly not an attempt at a definition of the origins of the material universe, as is claimed for Philolaus. Instead, it is quite clear that for Plato the *One* form (whether of wisdom or pleasure—neither of which is a material object) is considered the unlimited, and the *various expressions* of it are seen as limitedness, the expression of the form in the mundane world. Plato implies here what he clearly states elsewhere, namely that because this world is an imitation of the eternal one, and deals mainly with time, space, and materiality, the limited expressions of a form can never fully encapsulate its eternal archetype.

At the end of the procedure stated above in the quotation, Socrates says that only after distinguishing between the single form and the possible expressions of limitedness, can the intermediates be allowed to pass away into the unlimited, namely the single form.

The second point to be made is that all those scholars throughout history who have used Plato's single reference to limitedness and unlimited as a support or proof for a scientific and/or *material* origin of the universe, are clearly mistaken. That single statement in the *Philebus* needs to be weighed against *all* the dialogues up to the Republic wherein Plato has argued for the immortality of the soul; the law of necessity (karma) and of transmigration of the soul [reincarnation]—hardly doctrines connected with material origins of the universe! In fact, if we take Plato's *Timaeus,* as his version of the origin of the universe, we may note these words: "All men, Socrates, who have any degree of right feeling, at the beginning of every enterprise, whether small or great, always call upon God" (*Timaeus*, 27-c).

After discussing the eternal cause of our world, and stating that our world is a copy of the eternal cause, Timaeus goes on to state: "Let me tell you then why the creator made this world of generation. He was good, and the good can never have any jealousy of anything. So being free from jealousy, he desired that all things be as like himself as they could be.... God desired that all things should be good and nothing bad" (*Timaeus*, 28c–29e).

The case has been made that limiteds and unlimiteds do not have a Pythagorean source, but a Presocratic one. And we have reported that this position, (misrepresented as a Pythagorean doctrine) and blindly followed down the ages by scholars and commentators, is quite incorrect. One may surmise that by the time of Philolaus, the Pythagorean doctrines were so changed and possibly distorted by the passage of time and the events of history, that they no longer represented a true picture of Pythagoras' original teachings. The main example is that of material unlimiteds and limiters that replace the transcendental Monad and the undefined dyad as originating cosmic principles.

Another possible example of misinterpreted original teachings can be found in Plato's dialogue, *Phaedo*, dealing with the immortality of the soul. In that dialogue two protagonists are introduced, Cebes and Simmias, who are described as Pythagoreans. They ask Socrates a number of questions that relate to this idea of the soul's immortality (*Phaedo*, 84c-88b). At 86b, Simmias likens the soul to a musical instrument "where the instrument itself and its strings are material and corporeal and composite...while the attunement is invisible and incorporeal." Simmias goes on to tell Socrates: "We Pythagoreans have a theory of the soul which is roughly like this: The body is held together at a certain tension between the extremes of hot and cold, and dry and wet, and so on, and our soul is a temperament or adjustment of these same extremes, when they are combined in just the right proportion. Well, if the soul is really an adjustment, obviously as soon as the tension of our body is lowered or increased beyond the proper point, the soul must be destroyed" (*Phaedo*, 86b–d). These are not Pythagorean doctrines. Quite the opposite!

Cebes adds his vexations: "But as for (the soul) still existing somewhere after we are dead, I think that proof fails in this way" (*Phaedo*, 87). He gives the example of a tailor who makes a coat, asking: If the tailor died, which would be "likely to last longer, a man or a coat?" Cebes is concerned that even if the soul inhabited succeeding bodies [coats] he worries that at one of its "deaths" it would perish altogether. He concludes by saying "Socrates, no one but a fool is entitled to face death with confidence, unless he can prove that the soul is absolutely immortal and indestructible. Otherwise everyone must always feel apprehension at the approach of death." Here, again, Cebes is asking his questions from a mundane and temporal point of view.

The conclusion to be drawn from the encounter between Simmias and Cebes is that they are designated as Pythagorean, and yet they no longer possess the knowledge of the immortality of the soul that Pythagoras taught to his disciples, and which Plato taught to his pupils in the Academy. We can see for ourselves the deterioration of understanding on the part of those who still considered themselves Pythagoreans but were by then far removed from the essential transcendental teachings originally taught by Pythagoras.

This fact serves to confirm our judgment that Philolaus, too, had lost touch with, or misrepresented teachings from "Pythagoreans" into something that had no semblance whatsoever to the original. In fact, in the case of Philolaus, it seems his ultimate allegiance was with the Presocratics, and it seems likely that he therefore used Pythagorean doctrines to bolster his own individual views.

In reviewing the case for limiters and unlimiteds, it is clear that Philolaus' doctrines, such as they are, in no way correspond to the doctrines of Pythagoras as outlined in Alexander Polyhistor's document, which he claimed came from Pythagoras' memoirs. In fact, we must reluctantly conclude that Mr. Huffman has elaborated upon, or used wishful thinking in introducing some factors that simply are not found in Philolaus' original fragments (e.g., Aristotle's time, breath, void).

In addition, the terms limiters and unlimiteds, as Huffman has noted, have Presocratic origins. Either they have once again been misrepresented as Pythagorean terms, or Philolaus is so far removed from the original teachings that he didn't even know Pythagoras' chosen definitions were Monad and Undefined Dyad.

Finally, it is time we compared Aristotle and Philolaus. Aristotle is closer to the truth than Philolaus on the question of unlimited(s) and limiteds, but he does not possess it in Pythagoras' original form. Aristotle would concur with Pythagoras when he says the world is one, and he would concur when he describes the unlimited as a single principle (though for Pythagoras that principle is the transcendental Monad or

God, and for Aristotle God is the rather distant and remote Prime Mover). Note that there is no God or transcendental origin for Philolaus' Presocratic universe.

In Aristotle's astronomical system, the Prime Mover is at the outermost ring of the concentric circles of the cosmos, but He is turned away into His eternal realm and has nothing to do with life down on the Earth, much less a concern for His human creations. For Pythagoras and the Eastern philosophies/religions the Monad, God, creates the entire universe *out of himself.* He creates/inhabits the undefined dyad, and as Pythagoras says, the cosmos is a living being and every particle is filled with the energy and divinity of the Monad. Aristotle has vaguely grasped the concept of the Monad's emanation into matter, for he describes the unlimited—singular, a principle—as that from which the world drew time, breath, and void. But for Pythagoras it is not that the world drew *from* the unlimited time, breath, and void, as though the Monad was passive and the world the active principle; it is that the *Monad* breathed out the entire universe, and among the first emanations, was that which separates the eternal world from the mundane world, namely time and space, and the dualities.

Philolaus' cosmology is far less coherent than that of Aristotle. Philolaus had begun by stating, "Nature in the world order was *fitted together* both out of things which are unlimited and out of things which are limiting, both the world order as a whole and everything in it" (Huffman, 43).

First, for Pythagoras there is no hint that Nature was "fitted together." For Pythagoras *Nature,* the temporal universe is an emanation of the transcendental Monad into the material universe. The idea of the world being "fitted together," as if it were an automobile with many parts, would have been laughable to Pythagoras.

Second, there is no terminology in Pythagoras that corresponds to unlimited and limited. If a Platonic term may be applied here, it would be the designation of the One (transcendental) and the many (the many material, mundane expressions of the One in this world. The One is misunderstood *as matter* because matter creates a barrier between the many things and the One unless the senses, intellect, and soul are purified.

Third, for Philolaus the unlimiteds and limiters have a material source, in Nature; they are multiple, and the whole of the world-order is comprised of these unknown and undefined "bits" or "groups" of matter. Such an idea would also be quite laughable for Pythagoras.

Fourth, Philolaus declares that limiteds/unlimiteds are primary (beyond Aristotle's number) but the question is raised: How are material and originating limiteds and unlimiteds able to create both the central fire and the sphere which encloses it. Philolaus would have us believe that material, undesignated limiters and unlimiteds can create invisible elements such as the central fire and the counter-earth, an idea that is as laughable as it is incoherent.

In the end neither Aristotle nor Philolaus has a correct understanding of Pythagoras' cosmology, though Aristotle is closer in that he accepts the Prime Mover. Philolaus, creating a purely material universe of limiters and unlimiteds, demonstrates once again that he identifies with the Presocratic tradition, and the fact that his version of cosmology has been interpreted as that of Pythagoras, or the Pythagoreans is, once again, not only shown to be lamentably incorrect, but to have done enormous damage to the reputation of the ancient Pythagoreans who were taught the transcendental truth of the cosmos by Pythagoras himself.

Chapter 5

Number

Huffman starts out by stating, "An overview of the genuine fragments and testimonia of Philolaus reveals that he is not primarily a mathematician" (Huffman, 54), but that *plenty of interest* in mathematics is revealed (fragment 6a) of his knowledge of "whole-number ratios that govern concordant intervals in music. Testimoniam A24 *plausibly* shows he knew the musical proportions (12, 9, 8,6), "which in turn *presupposes* knowledge of the arithmetic and harmonic means. A29 and A7a *suggest* he recognized mathematical sciences—arithmetic, geometry, astronomy, and music—and, he even established a hierarchy of sciences with geometry as the basic science. In fragment 5 he presents a threefold classification of numbers and in fragment 4 he identifies numbers as the basis of our knowledge of reality. Huffman sees Philolaus as the "first thinker self-consciously and thematically to employ mathematical ideas to solve philosophical problems" (ibid., 54–55).

Philolaus is criticized by Burkert who claimed that his mathematics was more in line with Pythagorean mysticism than the more "rigorous deductive mathematics" of some of his contemporaries. And, Huffman challenges the Aristotelian view of Pythagoreans that all things *are* numbers, whereas Philolaus states that "things cannot be known *without* number, not that things *are* numbers" (ibid., 58).

Philolaus (ibid., 65) distinguishes the things of this world that can be known from the ultimate basis of reality which is beyond our grasp, and here sides with Empedocles, Anaxagoras, and the atomists "who assume the existence of the world of our experience, a world consisting of a plurality of things." And although Philolaus seems to share with some Presocratics "strong skepticism" about the reliability of our senses, in fragment 2 he did rely on "direct appeal to sense experience to establish the existence of limiters and unlimiteds" (ibid., 66).

However, Philolaus held some views that might seem surprising to one who has, thus far, espoused Presocratic doctrines. Apparently he felt that it was crucial to go beyond the superficial messages of the senses, and employs number in order to arrive at a proper interpretation of things. For Philolaus, "individual things in the world 'give signs of' or 'point to' something else, not in this case the logos of Heraclitus, but...numbers or 'forms of numbers.'" Huffman emphasizes that Philolaus' notion that things in the material world point to numbers for interpretation and explanation, is a "very original response" to an epistemological question posed by "the most illustrious of his predecessors, Parmenides" (ibid., 67).

Basically, that epistemological question was what counts as proof of an object of knowledge. To contextualize Parmenides' own response to this question, one must bear in mind that in his poem, *On Nature,* he posits a division between the eternal world of *what is,* and the material world (which he completely rejects) as *what is not.* Thus, for Parmenides "an object of inquiry must be uncreated and imperishable, continuous, unchangeable and perfect" (ibid., 67). He rejected the route of *what is not* because it was "completely indeterminate, and hence incurably vague."

Huffman claims that Philolaus provided a most original answer to Parmenides by accepting Parmenides' dictum that the "object of knowledge must be in a determinate (as opposed to an indeterminate) state of affairs" but he argued that "numerical relationships in particular and mathematical relationships in general, solve the problem. They possess the requisite determinacy, and at the same time they relate a plurality of entities, and thus are capable of explaining a world that consists of a plurality of entities" (ibid.).

Huffman refers to examples of requisite determinacy (reliable proof) as follows: "If we consider a geometrical proof such as the so-called Pythagorean theorem [Euclid, 1:47] or the numerical proportions that govern the concordant intervals in the octave they do in fact seem to be uncreated and imperishable." Where the particular instance of concordant intervals—i.e.:

Two particular taut strings, one twice the length of the other, may come to be and pass away, but it seems quite plausible to argue that ½, ⅔, and ¾ and concordant sounds, or the relationship between the hypotenuse and sides of a right angle, did not come into existence at any point, nor will they pass away. Similarly there seems little problem in saying that mathematical relationships are unchangeable. Further, since mathematical relationships are completely determinate, they are perfect in Parmenides' sense of being complete and not deficient." (ibid., 68)

Philolaus' mathematical solution to Parmenides important epistmological question is put in context by comparing it with the Presocratic solution offered by the atomists, "often seen as positing a plurality of entities which individually satisfy the requirements of Parmenidean being." Clearly Philolaus rejects that solution. For him "the world is known through number, not made up of number" (ibid.). Huffman reminds us, however, that "the basic principles in Philolaus' system are not numbers but limiters and unlimiteds" (ibid., 69).

Huffman tells us that "'having number' as equivalent to 'having an order or structure that can be specified in terms of the relationship between numbers.' To say that something 'has number' then becomes equivalent to saying that it has a structure which can be described in terms of mathematics" (ibid., 70).

At this point Huffman introduces Aristotle into the discussion, saying he suggested that mathematics held an epistemological role for the Pythagoreans:

> The Pythagoreans having devoted themselves to mathematics, and admiring the accuracy of its reasonings, because it alone among human activities knows of proofs, and seeing the facts about harmony, that they happen on account of numbers, generally admitted...they deemed these [facts of mathematics] and their principles to be, generally, causative of existing things, so that whoever wishes to comprehend the true nature of existing things should turn his attention to these, that is to numbers and proportions, because it is by them that everything is made clear. (Iamblichus, Burkert, ibid.)

What Huffman finds remarkable about this passage is that in the beginning it is speaking about particular mathematical proofs, but "it ends up saying that to understand things we must study number and proportion. The study of number has become equivalent to the study of the structure of the cosmos insofar as it can be expressed in mathematical relationships" (ibid., 71).

Huffman posits, however, that "Philolaus is arguing that we really understand something only when we understand the structure of and relationships between its various parts. The best example is our understanding of the octave.... We can understand it only when we can specify the intervals...and the relationship between those intervals and can express them in terms of numerical ratios" (ibid., 70). Huffman claims no previous Presocratic had dared to invoke number as an explanatory concept, and that what is revolutionary in the "philosophy of Philolaus is the thematic use of number and mathematics to solve philosophical problems." As for Philolaus' doctrines on number:

Fragment 4: "And indeed all the things that are known have number. For it is not possible that anything whatsoever be understood without this."

Huffman then moves on (from Stobaeus, ibid., 177) and presents Philolaus' "threefold classification of numbers":

Fragment 5 "Number, indeed, has two proper kinds, odd and even, and a third from both mixed together, the even–odd. Of each of the two kinds there are many forms, of which each thing itself gives signs" (ibid., 178).

However, in discussing the authenticity of the fragment Huffman tells us, "Aristotle reports that the Pythagoreans thought that the even and the odd were the elements of number and that the one was from both of these and was thus both even and odd" (*Meta I*, 5 986a 17-20). Huffman continues that Aristotle posited that the Pythagoreans had "in a similar manner to others, proposed two first principles," but where Huffman would have expected these two first principles to be even and odd, "what we get is the assertion that the unlimited and the limit are the two Pythagorean principles" (Huffman, 179). Huffman continues that probably Aristotle meant to equate the unlimited as the even and the limit as the odd (ibid., 180). He also mentions that, in *Physics 3:4*, Aristotle "concludes by asserting that for the Pythagoreans the unlimited is even, and then goes on to assert that the even entrapped by the odd, gives things their unlimitedness. Thus Aristotle once again shifts to the even as the most basic principle used to explain the unlimited aspect of things (ibid.).

Huffman chides Aristotle for "overemphasis on the role of number and on the role of even and odd as the principles of all things, at the expense of the role of limiters and unlimiteds which Aristotle's own text shows to have been commonly accepted Pythagorean first principles" (ibid., 188–181).

As I have pointed out in my book on Plato, I believe Aristotle seriously misinterpreted Pythagorean numbers. But if Aristotle based the above ideas on those he had inherited from Philolaus, then we must wonder whether Philolaus was not the *cause* of Aristotle's misinterpretation of Pythagorean numbers.

My point is that fragment 5 is attributed to Stobaeus not Philolaus, and, if it *is* claimed for Philolaus, as his "threefold classification of numbers" (i.e., odd, even, and a third, even–odd), it reveals that his doctrine of numbers, as well as that of Aristotle, has absolutely nothing in common with that of Pythagoras.

One argument is that there can be no numbers that are odd–even because odd and even are *categories* of numbers, and one can not add or subtract categories of numbers. Huffman points out that Aristotle found a connection between odd numbers and limiters and even numbers and unlimiteds. And I would reply that when adding numbers (even if they are standing in for classification of numbers as odd, even, and a mixture of the two, odd–even) you need to specify a *particular* odd number and a particular even number in order to mix (i.e., add) them together. If you add the first two numbers 1 and 2, (which apparently, to Philolaus and Aristotle represent designations of odd and even) they will never add up to a "one that is both even *and* odd," but will by simple mathematical logic, add up to three.

One notes here that fragment 5 says that of the individual categories of odd and even, there are many forms, but no mention is made of a single example of odd–even, which perhaps confirms that in mathematical terms, Philolaus *discovered* none. In addition, if it is true that Aristotle equated limiters with even and unlimiteds with odd, then he has generalized Philolaus' plural and material originating constituents of reality, limiters and unlimiteds into two principles, and out of these two principles he has derived a *one*. Or, should we assume that when Aristotle is referring to the Pythagoreans with regard to number, he was in fact basing his number doctrines on those he derived from Philolaus? In which case, as I have posited, they both were mistaken if we compare their number systems to that of Pythagoras.

As researchers, we might have assumed that from these two originating principles, limiters and unlimiteds, there was produced a *one* that was the beginning of the number system (for them), but since it is designated as even *and* odd, that designation will not suffice. Nor indeed is it *possible* that out of material principles a number system will arise.

From a commonsense point of view there can be no number that is both odd and even. It might have made sense to Philolaus who held that the origins of the universe were *two groups of material things*, the limiters and unlimiteds, that needed to be fit together by a third term, the harmonia, but not to Pythagoras.

We must emphasize here that, for Philolaus, limiters and unlimiteds produce the *one*.... Aristotle refers to this, which would imply that two *material* principles produce the *one* that is the beginning of the number series, despite the fact that it is described as odd and even. Nor would it explain how that number series could be applied to its own originating multiple principles, limiters and unlimiteds.

Such a confusing philosophical statement clearly does not apply to the doctrine of Pythagoras as outlined by Alexander Polyhistor. "The principle of all things is the Monad or Unit; arising from this Monad the undefined dyad, or Two serves as material substratum to the Monad which is cause."

As Polyhistor's quotation shows, the Monad is defined as One, and the undefined dyad, the material substratum as Two. Thus, I take the number series in Pythagoras to be coexistent with the Monad and undefined dyad, and that One and Two also refer to principles that manifest the entire universe, as the next statement clearly confirms: "From the Monad *and* the undefined dyad spring numbers." Thus, it is the *relation* between these two principles that produces numbers. (There is, however, a mystery here because a dyad is defined as two aspects of something (in this case, reality) which cannot be considered as existentially different from one another, except that here the Monad, One, is transcendental, and the undefined dyad, or Two, is the entire material universe. It is interesting to note that Parmenides, who divided the universe into *what is* (i.e., eternal, and *what is not*, i.e., the material world), described *what is* as determinate, (i.e., one could make reliable statements about it), and he described the material world as indeterminate—i.e., one could make no truly reliable statements about it.

It is perhaps coincidental that Pythagoras referred to the material substratum, the material world as the undefined dyad, whereas Plato's term "indefinite dyad" could well parallel Parmenides' term *indeterminate*. But where Parmenides clearly rejected the material world, the nature of Pythagoras' undefined dyad was that it was an integral and internal principle of the Monad, in fact it was bound to the Monad as the other half of its very being! What this implies is that our very universe is comprised of and saturated by the divine Monad, and that we do not recognize it. Perhaps, too, that is why Plato said that our world is a copy of the eternal one and why "time is the moving image of eternity."

However, moving forward, Alexander Polyhistor has told us that from the Monad and undefined dyad spring numbers. The progression that follows must have been completely unheard of in the ancient Greek world, for in deceptively simple terms it describes the logical and mathematical emanation of the transcendental Monad through various dimensions until it arrives at the final density which represents our material world, or perhaps more correctly, our cosmos, a term Pythagoras is credited with coining. That progression is as follows:

> from numbers arose points
> from points arose lines
> from lines arose plane figures
> from plane figures arose solid figures
> from solid figures arose sensible bodies

elements of sensible bodies are four—fire, water, earth and air these elements interchange and turn into one another.

To envisage this cosmic emanation correctly, we must be sure to view each new progression, i.e., from lines to plane figures, for example, as an entire *dimension* that represents a well-known mathematical progression, but applied to the emerging density of the cosmos. As one can imagine, the evolution of the cosmos, took untold *aeons* in its journey to arrive at the dense matter we on this Earth call the material world.

When we compare this cosmically mathematical progression of the Monad, and undefined dyad, into matter, with the notion of Philolaus that the universe arose from two opposing groups of material principles, and had to be brought into the world order by the harmonia, it reveals once again that Philolaus' cosmology has absolutely nothing in common with that of Pythagoras. It also appears that his number system is a philosophical, and incoherent, construct, and bears no resemblance to the simplicity, elegance, and harmony of Pythagoras' exposition of how numbers provide the mathematical structure of our universe.

TETRAKTYS

One of the more difficult mathematical doctrines of Pythagoras concerns what is described as the tetraktys. David Fideler, who wrote the introduction to the *Pythagorean Sourcebook and Library,* compiled and translated by Kenneth Sylvan Guthrie, explains on page 28: "Through their investigation of musical harmony, the Pythagoreans shifted philosophic inquiry away from the materialistic cosmologies of the earlier Ionic tradition to the consideration of Form, which was now to be seen as constituting the world of First Principles."

"The Pythagoreans perceived another principle of Number, in addition to seeing it as a formative agent in nature. This is perhaps best exemplified in the figure of the Tetraktys which, as we might say in the present century, stood as the "numerical paradigm of whole systems." It consisted "of the first four integers arranged in a triangle of ten points"(ibid., 28).

For the Pythagoreans the Tetraktys symbolized the perfection of Number and the elements that comprise it. In one sense it would be proper to say that the Tetraktys symbolizes, like the musical scale, a differentiated image of Unity; in the case of the Tetraktys, it is an image of unity starting at One, proceeding through four levels of manifestation, and returning to unity, i.e., Ten. In the sphere of geometry....

One represents the point. Two represents the line.
Three represents the plane. Four represents the first 3-D form.

Hence, in the realm of space, the Tetraktys represents the continuity linking the dimensionless point with the manifestation of the first body; the figure of the Tetraktys itself also represents the vertical hierarchy of relation between Unity and emerging Multiplicity. In the realm of music, it will be seen that the Tetraktys also contains the symphonic ratios that underlie the mathematical harmony of the musical scale: 1:2, the octave; 2:3 the perfect fifth; and 3:4, the perfect fourth [which add up to ten].

We might further note that the Tetraktys, being a Triangular number, is composed of consecutive integers, incorporating both the odd and even, whereas Square number is comprised of odd integers, and Oblong, the number of consecutive even integers. Since the universe is comprised of peras and apeiron woven together through mathematical harmonia, it is easy to see from these considerations why the Tetraktys, or the Decad, was called Kosmos (world-order), Ouranos (heaven) and Pan

(the All). In Pythagorean thought the Tetraktys came to represent an inclusive paradigm of the fourfold pattern which underlies different classes of phenomena, as exemplified by Theon of
Smyrna in appendix I. Not only does a fourfold pattern underlie each class, but each level is in a certain fashion analogous
or proportionately similar with that same level in every other
class of phenomena.... The Pythagoreans, then, were the first
to use numerical and geometrical diagrams of cosmic wholeness
and the celestial order....thus illustrating the principle of unity
underlying diversity. (ibid., pp. 29–30)

I would add my own simplified version of the Tetraktys as follows:
One symbolizes cosmic unity, the Monad, before manifestation occurs.
Two symbolizes the indefinite dyad, the material universe. *Three* symbolizes the relation, or union, between One and Two. *Four* symbolizes
the multiplicity of forms that they create through their endless relations
and permutations. The Chinese call it the "ten thousand things." I will
let the reader decide which version of the Tetraktys appeals most to
your sensibilities, but I would note that, first, Fideler is still referring
to these mathematical doctrines as "Pythagorean" when, as Heath has
attested, they are clearly the achievements of a great genius, Pythagoras himself.

Since the *Pythagorean Sourcebook and Library* was published in
1987, I would have expected Fideler to have more accurately defined the
source of paradigm-shifting mathematical theories affecting the entire
cosmos, as being attributed to Pythagoras. And I note that he, too, is
describing mathematical phenomena in the Tetraktys as representing
limit and unlimited, terms I believe to have come into manifestation
in later generations of interpreters who were no longer in touch with
original doctrines of Pythagoras himself. *His* doctrines are aligned
with and an outgrowth of Eastern philosophies and religions, including Hinduism and Buddhism, as Édouard Schuré points out.

THE MEANING OF TEN

In this connection I would like to quote from Thomas Heath (*History
of Greek Mathematics,* 75–76): "While for Euclid, Theon of Smyrna,

and the Neo-Pythagoreans the 'perfect' number was the kind of number above described":

fifth, $2^{12} (2^{13} - 1) = 33\ 550\ 336$

sixth, $2^{16} (2^{17} - 1) = 8\ 589\ 869\ 056$

seventh, $2^{18} (2^{19} - 1) = 137\ 438\ 691\ 328$

eighth, $2^{30} (2^{31} - 1) = 2\ 305\ 843\ 008\ 139\ 952\ 128$

ninth, $2^{60} (2^{61} - 1) = 2\ 658\ 455\ 991\ 569\ 831\ 744\ 654\ 692$
$$615\ 953\ 842\ 176$$

tenth, $2^{88} (2^{89} - 1)$.

"Perfect" numbers (Heath, A History of Greek Mathematics)

We are told that the Pythagoreans made 10 the perfect number. Aristotle says that this was because they found within it such things as the void, proportion, oddness, and so on [*Meta.* M. 811084 a 32–34]. The reason is explained more in detail by Theon of Smyrna (p. 93. 17-94.9) and in the fragment of Speusippus. [The number] 10 is the sum of the numbers 1, 2, 3, 4 forming the tetraktys ("their greatest oath," ... the "principle of health." These numbers include the ratios corresponding to the musical intervals discovered by Pythagoras, namely 4:3 (the fourth) 3:2 (the fifth), and 2:1 (the octave). Speusippus observes further that 10 contains in it the "linear," "plane," and "solid" varieties of number; or 1 is a point, 2 is a line, 3 a triangle, and four a pyramid" (Heath, *History of Greek Mathematics,* 75–76).

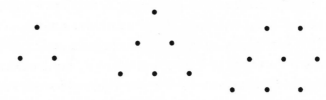

Diagram of dots

This, then, is one more explanation of what Pythagoras may have meant by his seemingly humble diagram of little dots. They were a mathematical replication of the evolution of the Monad into matter, by carefully calculated stages, in which each represented a deeper level

density. It is most definitely not what Philolaus and/or
e speculated upon—that it referred, in strange and fanciful
e planetary system of our cosmos where Pythagoreans sup-
p. "made up" planets to arrive at a "proper total of ten." Pythagoras would have said, "What kind of science is that!"

Indeed, the paradigm-shifting discoveries of Pythagoras inspire
both awe and wonder in the discerning reader. As Édouard Schuré
puts it,

From a higher point of view, when opened with the keys of comparative esotericism, his doctrine presents a magnificent composite, a solid whole, whose parts are bound by a fundamental
concept. In it we find a rational reproduction of the esoteric
doctrine of India and Egypt, to which he gave clarity and Hel-
lenistic simplicity, adding a more forceful feeling and a more
exact idea of human freedom.

At the same time and in various parts of the globe, great
reformers were making similar doctrines more generally known.
In China, Lao-Tse departed from the esotericism of Fo-Hi;
the last Buddha, Sakya-Moni was preaching on the banks of
the Ganges; in Italy the Etruscan priesthood sent an initiate
to Rome. This initiate was King Numa, who, armed with the
Sybilline Books, sought to restrain the threatening ambition of
the Roman Senate by wise institutions. And it is not by chance
that these great reformers appear at the same time among such
different peoples. Their various missions are united in a common goal. They prove that at certain times a single spiritual current mysteriously passes through all humankind. Where does it
come from? From that divine world which is beyond our sight,
but whose seers and prophets are its ambassadors and witnesses.
(Schuré, 269–270)

For those interested in a rendition of Pythagoras' life that includes
his unknown higher spiritual doctrines, this book is an invaluable key.

NOTE ON NUMBER

One final point needs to be mentioned about Number. It is a tool, and an explanation, but it is not the be-all and end-all of cosmology. Mathematics is, as Pythagoras first revealed, the language by which we describe and explain the world. As an example, when Albert Einstein was working on the theory of relativity, his intention was not to give the highest honor to the most famous equation in the world: E=mc squared. No. That most famous equation describes and explains his momentous *discovery* that matter and energy were of the same "stuff" and therefore were interchangeable. And Pythagoras, to whom is attributed the most famous theorem in history, the Pythagorean theorem, was not only the first scientist in the West to disseminate geometry, number, the musical intervals, the heliocentric theory, and the harmony of the spheres, but he was also the first to use the discipline of mathematics as the very language by which to describe the cosmos.

Nonetheless, in my judgment it is a mistake to obsess overly much on the aspect of number—important as it is in its own domain—but what is important is to realize its greater goal is to reveal to us mysteries of the cosmos that would have remained hidden or concealed without such revelations. In the case of Pythagoras, the Monad was all. God was All. Number was in the Monad, which he describes as the One, the Unity of things. The structure of the cosmos is described by the language of mathematics but ultimately it is the divine Monad that contains *All,* including number.

CHAPTER 6

HARMONIA

The major philosophical problem before Philolaus is how to "fit together" his two major, undefined groups of principles, limiters and unlimiteds. Huffman tells us that in the second half of fragment 6 Philolaus argues "that limiters and unlimiteds are essentially unlike and would never come to form an ordered whole unless some third principle bound them together. This principle is known as *harmonia,* or 'fitting together'" (Huffman, 73). Huffman tells us that "what is new in Philolaus is the fact that he *almost* identifies harmonia with number."

After Huffman has introduced the concept of harmonia in fragment 6 he immediately goes on to discuss it in quantitative terms (he refers to its size) and that turns upon a discussion of the system of whole-number ratios that determine a diatonic scale. "In fact, the first actual numbers we meet in the fragments of Philolaus are this system of ratios that is said to determine the size of the harmonia of the cosmos" (ibid., 73). Here, Huffman seems to have completely forgotten that the discovery of the numerical intervals making up the octave (2:1); the perfect fourth (4:3), and the perfect fifth (3:2), and the *means* that obtained between numerical relations were all attributed by Heath to Pythagoras. Therefore, these ideas of Philolaus are not original, and, we must bear in mind that the philosophical problem for Pythagoras was how *would* such musical intervals apply to the external cosmos.

Huffman explains, "Insofar as he (Philolaus) is trying to present us with the truth about the world order and the individual things in it, his treatment of cosmogony, astronomy, psychology, and medicine should show him at least *searching* for the numbers in things, just as Plato said that the Pythagoreans searched for numbers in heard harmonies"

(*Republic*, 531 C1-2). Here Huffman implies that the Pythagoreans *searched* for numbers in heard harmonies, whereas the exact quote from the *Republic* is that "their method exactly corresponds to that of the astronomers, for the numbers they seek are those *found* in heard concords." Since Pythagoras had discovered those concords, and obviously taught his students of the consonances between the musical intervals and the musical structure of the entire cosmos, his students were confirming those numbers, whereas it is my view that Philolaus was merely groping for them. The stark truth is that since he was not a mathematician/astronomer and could not and did not discover the *scientific* consonances between the planets, he would *never* have been able to apply his harmonia to the cosmos. His harmonia is nothing but a fairytale.

However, further investigation of Philolaus' harmonia is required. Thus, the third term, so crucial in "fitting together" the unlimiteds and limiters into the world order, is described in fragment 6a: "But since these beginnings preexisted and were neither alike or even related, it would have been impossible for them to be ordered if a harmony had not come upon them, in whatever way it came to be. Like things and related did not, in addition require any harmony, but things that are unlike and not even related nor of [the same speed?], it is necessary that such things be bonded together by a harmony if they are going to be held in an order" (Huffman, 124).

Huffman interprets this fragment as meaning that these beginnings, namely the unlimiteds and limiteds, preexisted, meaning they preexisted in the world of Nature because they were both material in origin. And, because they were not related to one another—i.e., were in opposition to one another, it would have been impossible for them to be part of the world order if a harmony had not come upon them, whatever way it came to be. Here we may be surprised, even perplexed, at Philolaus' apparent inability to know the source of the harmony. And he has told us that only the unlike or unrelated things must be bonded together by a harmony in order to become part of the world order, since the things that are alike are already in harmony.

Let us underscore at the outset that Philolaus' *harmonia* and material world order appear to be in direct opposition to the doctrines of Pythagoras, whose single, transcendental Monad, the One unfolds or creates the material world of Nature from itself. And since the Monad is described as One and a Unity, it therefore contains within itself the world order and all numbers (in potentiality if we prefer the Aristotelian term, but necessarily adapted to transcendental cosmological origins and their evolution into matter). For Pythagoras the Monad is eternal, and Nature is its material extension and counterpart.

For Philolaus the limiters and unlimiteds—whatever they may be—are material, without a specific origin, and all that is known of them is that some of them, the ones which are unlike and unrelated to the others, require a harmony—however that may occur—in order for a necessary world order to prevail. For Pythagoras the world order pre-exists eternally in the Monad, whereas for Philolaus it arrives, unannounced, "out of numbers" and it is their harmony that is needed to impose world order on the originating material constituents of existence, the limiters and unlimiteds, specifically those which are *unlike* and which *need* to be incorporated into the world order.

First of all, we must bear in mind that Huffman had begun his investigation by pointing out that "an overview of the genuine fragments and testimonia of Philolaus reveals that he is *not primarily* a *mathematician*" (Huffman, 54). He further posited that Philolaus' *interest in* mathematics was revealed by various fragments and testimonia. He points to fragment 6a—penned by Nicomachus (AD 60–100), and preserved by Stobaeus (fifth century AD)—as revealing Philolaus' knowledge of "whole-number ratios that govern concordant intervals in music" (ibid.). In fact, Nicomachus actually begins by stating:

> The most ancient thinkers also proclaimed things that are consistent with what I have set forth. They call the octave *harmonia*, the fourth *syllaba*…the fifth *dioxeion*…and the octave is the composite of both the *syllaba* [fourth] and *dioxeion* [fifth] (for this very reason called *harmonia* because it was the first concord fitted together [*harmosthe*] from concords). Philolaus, the successor of Pythagoras makes this clear when he says something like the following in the first book of *On Nature*" (ibid. 146)

Nichomachus then refers to the "text of Philolaus" which describes in technical terms the relationship between octave, fourth, and fifth (ibid.).

Several things jump out here. First that the fragment is attributed to Nicomachus, not Philolaus himself. Second that he refers to "ancient thinkers" who have also dealt with the octave, fourth , fifth, and harmonia. Third, the harmonia was defined as the *octave*—so called because it was the first concord fitted together from other concords. And fourth, that Philolaus is described as "the successor of Pythagoras."

Next, Huffman referring to Testimoniam A24, under the heading "Number and Harmonia," says Philolaus "is plausibly said to have known the 'musical proportions' (12, 9, 8, 6), which in turn presupposes knowledge of the arithmetic and harmonic means" (ibid., 54). Again, Testimoniam A24 is not penned by Philolaus, but by Nicomachus (with a secondary input from Iamblichus). It states, "Testimonium A24: Some, following Philolaus, believe that it [the mean] is called harmonic from its attendance on all geometric harmony.... They say that it (musical proportion) is a discovery of the Babylonians and *through Pythagoras* first came to the Greeks" (ibid., 168).

In the section on Authenticity, Huffman speaks of three "means" and says "the first three means are said to have been known by Pythagoras, or his followers, Plato, and Aristotle" (ibid.). Let us reiterate what is clearly stated by Nicomachus and Iamblichus: that the notion of musical proportion (including the three means—arithmetic, geometric, and harmonic) first came to the Greeks through Pythagoras.

Huffman continues by stating that Testimonia "A29 and A7a, *suggest* he [Philolaus] *recognized* mathematical sciences—arithmetic, geometry, astronomy, and music—and that "he even established a hierarchy of sciences with geometry as the basic science" (ibid., 54). In fact, Testimoniam A29, attributed to Sextus Empiricus (AD 160–210), is about the supremacy of mathematical reason.

Testimonium A29: "Anaxagoras said that reason in general was the criterion. The Pythagoreans said that reason was the criterion but not reason in general, but rather the reason that arises from the mathematical sciences, just as Philolaus also said" (ibid., 199). Here Sextus Empiricus is clearly talking about what constitutes proof for an object of knowledge. What is interesting is that while he attributes mathematical reason to the Pythagoreans, he adds "just as Philolaus also said"—a statement that seems to imply Philolaus was not part of the

Pythagoreans, but had also agreed with them regarding the supremacy of mathematical reason in determining proof of an object of knowledge.

In addition, Testimoniam A7a, by Plutarch, is about the supremacy of geometry: "Geometry being, as Philolaus says, the source and the mother-city of the rest of the mathematical sciences."

Regarding fragment 6, attributed to Stobaeus, Huffman tells us that as to the source of harmony, Philolaus did not seem to know where it would arise or how it would come to be. However, if we hearken back to fragment 6a, we see that Nichomachus is positing some very *specific* aspects of the harmonia:

> The magnitude of harmonia (fitting together) is the fourth (*syllaba*) and the fifth (*di' oxeian*). The fifth is greater than the fourth by the ratio of 9:8 (a tone). For the hypate (lowest tone) to the middle string (*mese*) is a fourth, and from the middle string to *neate* (highest tone) is a fifth, but from neate to the third string is a fourth, and from the third string to hypate is a fifth. That which is in between the third string and the middle string is in the ratio of 9:8 [a tone], the fourth has the ratio 4:3, the fifth 3:2, and the octave (*diapason*) 2:1. Thus, the harmonia is five 9:8 ratios [tones] and two *dieses* [smaller semitones]; the fifth is three 9:8 ratios [tones] and a *dieses*; and the fourth two 9:8 ratios (tones) and a *diesis*.
>
> One should bear in mind that at this point he calls the string in the seven-string scale which is next to the middle string (*paramese*), the third string, before the insertion of the disjunct tone in the eight-string scale. For this note [*trite paramese*] used to be an undivided tone and a half from the string that is next to *nete* (*paranete*) from which the inserted string took away a tone; the remaining half-tone was left between the third string and the one next to the middle (*paramese*) in the disjunct scale. (ibid., 146–147)

Nicomachus is telling us the insertion of note trite is *into an eight-note disjunct scale*, whereas this disjunction did not occur in the seven-string version. Some thought that the change made it impossible for the third string to be at a ratio of 4:3 from *nete*. And others said that the inserted note was not between the middle string and the third string, but between the third string and the string that is *next* to *nete* (*paramete*). They also say that it was called the third string in place of that one, and that the ancient third string became the string next to the middle in the disjunct scale. Nichomachus closes by saying, "And they say that Philolaus called the string next to the middle by *the earlier name*, third string, although it was a fourth from *nete*" (ibid., 147)

This passage seems to indicate that there was some controversy between those who held to an earlier seven-string version of musical relationships, or ratios, and those who had inserted another string, making an eight-string version, which introduced a disjunct note into the scale. And Nicomachus tells us, there is some lack of clarity regarding the placement of the string next to the third string, which he, Philolaus calls by its earlier name, third string, although it was a fourth away from *nete*—which would change the ratios. See diagram:

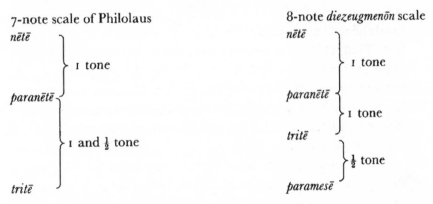

7-note scale of Philolaus

nētē

1 tone

paranētē

1 and ½ tone

tritē

8-note *diezeugmenōn* scale

nētē

1 tone

paranētē

1 tone

tritē

½ tone

paramesē

Seven-note and eight-note scales (Huffman, 155)

At the very least, Nicomachus' comments reveal a possible schism between those employing the seven-string scale and others who were advocating an eight-string scale with a disjunct note (the trite note). If Philolaus had discovered the musical intervals, surely he should have known which string represents which musical interval on the eight-string lyre.

As we shall see, it was Nicomachus who stated that *Pythagoras* introduced the eight-stringed lyre, which would reflect his knowledge of the octave with its eight notes. It is also likely that the change from a seven-string lyre, with its particular musical intervals—to the eight-stringed lyre, with its changed musical ratios reflects a subtle, but significant evolution of Greek consciousness. The preceeding discussion might seem somewhat tedious, but which *version* of the scale Philolaus accepted has great implications, since he reserves a cosmological application for it?

It is also important to note that in the discussion under the heading Authenticity (of fragment 6a), Huffman makes the following comment: "The later tradition, beginning as early as Xenocrates (fragment 9) ascribed the discovery of the ratios corresponding to the concordant intervals (2:1 = octave; 4:3 = fourth; 3:2 = fifth) to Pythagoras himself" (ibid., 147). However, Huffman says that a person called Lausus of Hermione (sixth century BC) knew these ratios and he was not a Pythagorean. He also mentions Hippasus doing an experiment that confirmed the ratios, and he rejects the story of how Pythagoras "heard" the intervals by saying such observations were impossible. Huffman concludes that it is uncertain whether knowledge of the ratios goes back to Pythagoras himself.

However, *we* may find some clarity on this issue by turning to the Commentary section of fragment 6a, where Huffman merely notes that "Nicomachus quotes fragment 6a without any hint as to its context in Philolaus' book." For the record, Nicomachus of Gerasa was considered an important ancient mathematician, author of the first important treatise on music theory since Aristoxenus and Euclid. He wrote several books on mathematics, now lost, but Nicomachus' *Enchiridion* (handbook) is a brief treatise on some basic points in harmonics.

One feature of the *Enchiridion* is that it focuses on the achievements of Pythagoras himself. In section five, *he is introduced as the person who added the eighth string to the seven-string lyre.* In section six we are given the story of Pythagoras' discovery of the ratios of whole numbers that correspond to the concordant intervals. Finally in section seven Nicomachus presents the structure of the diatonic scale as Pythagoras' discovery (with the promise that his work with the enharmonic and chromatic scales will be discussed later (ibid., 156).

Huffman continues: Philolaus is introduced (in fragment 6a) to show that the ancients "proclaimed things consistent with what I have set forth." What is quoted from Philolaus has to do with the structure of the diatonic scale, and Nicomachus is using the quotation as support for what he said in section seven about *Pythagoras'* construction of the diatonic scale. Nicomachus' account of Pythagoras' construction of the diatonic scale is supported by confirming that one of his successors, Philolaus, used the same scale.

Levin challenges the notion that Philolaus was a direct pupil of Pythagoras, but Huffman says that the term need only mean "that Philolaus is a *follower* of Pythagoras," noting that Nichomachus sees Philolaus' harmonia as a clear example of the early diatonic scale. Huffman's conclusion is that Nichomachus' interpretation of fragment 6a "has nothing to do with the diatonic scale and is instead concerned to show the necessity of *harmonia as a basic principle in Philolaus' system*, along with limiters and unlimiteds." This interpretation requires *much* consideration, since it appears to be clarifying the difference between the seven-stringed lyre and a new eight-stringed lyre, where the numerical intervals would obviously be changed by the introduction of the new eighth string. But it appears somewhat cavalier for Huffman to ignore the content of fragment 6a which quite clearly refers to the relation of the musical intervals in the seven-stringed lyre to those comprising the eight-stringed lyre.

For Nichomachus, it was true that Pythagoras discovered the musical intervals, octave, fourth and fifth, as is now historically and universally accepted; it was *Pythagoras* who discovered the diatonic scale and, it was *Pythagoras* who added the eighth string in order to create the eight-note diatonic scale, with all that it implies.

In addition, Nicomachus spells out the structure of the diatonic scale in Fr 6a and states that Philolaus, the successor of Pythagoras, says something *like* the following in the first book *On Nature:* The conclusion here is that Philolaus could not have known the musical intervals or the eight-note diatonic scale without having received them directly or indirectly from Pythagoreans. And when Nichomachus refers to the "most ancient thinkers" he must have had clearly in his mind the achievements of the legendary Pythagoras.

One interesting aspect of fragment 6a is that Nicomachus states that the reason the term octave (i.e., *harmonia*) existed was not only that it was a composite from the musical intervals of the fourth and fifth, but also because it was the first concord fitted together from concords.

Is it coincidental that Nicomachus uses the term *fitted together* when confirming that it was the composite of the fourth and the fifth musical intervals that comprised the harmonia, or octave?

One cannot resist speculating that Philolaus was cognizant of this term, *fitted together,* and perhaps found a new and novel way in which to apply it to the structure of the universe! However, we must always bear in mind that in so doing, Philolaus was applying it to his multiple, material, undefined, principles of unlimitedness and limit, whereas for Pythagoras, the application is tied to the cosmic source of the universe, the transcendental Monad, and the mathematical structure of the universe which was seen as the expression of those transcendent principles in the world of Nature. Here, we may distinguish the Master, Pythagoras, from the student, or follower, Philolaus.

Be that as it may, Huffman is telling us that in Fr 6a Philolaus had adopted the fourth and the fifth as comprising the diatonic octave, and implies he was eager to make it apply to his originating principles of limiters and unlimiteds (ibid., 147).

Huffman claims as a result of the information provided by Pythagoras' diatonic scale (which Philolaus adopted) it was plausible to see the undefined continuum of possible musical pitches as the unlimited(s) and that the limiters would be the boundaries we establish in this continuum by picking out specific pitches. The example he gives is of a monochord where the indefinite number of pitches would symbolize the unlimited whereas the stops placed along it, namely specific pitches, would correspond to limiters. Huffman also makes clear that it was Philolaus' intention to apply this diatonic scale and the musical intervals to his cosmological model and that, owing to this achievement, he would be the first to apply mathematical solutions to philosophical problems. Huffman had also told us that "limiters and unlimiteds alone will not produce an ordered system...not just any set of pitches will produce a musically ordered set, such a set only results when the unlimited continuum is in accordance with number" (ibid., 90).

Clearly the pleasing set of pitches turned out to be the fourth and the fifth, which produced what the ancient thinkers referred to as harmonia, the octave. The greater point to be made here is that once the diatonic scale had been discovered, by Pythagoras according to Nich-omachus, it could be applied. Philolaus himself applied it in his example of the monochord. But let us emphasize, despite the fact that the pleas-ing notes on the monochord are specified, singled out from an infinite number of possible notes, the music in this case is a closed system—i.e., the unlimiteds and limiters are all found on a single monochord.

However, Philolaus faces a far more difficult problem applying his musical principles to the *universe,* because he has been shown by Huff-man not to have defined what he meant by *limiters* and *unlimiters,* nor even to have given a single example of them. In the musical example we see clearly the relation between the unlimited possibility of notes on the continuum that is limited by the various stops or notes on the string. But in the real world Philolaus has no unlimiteds that are defined, and thus he has no way to produce the limits, the stops or notes, that will specifically determine what his limiters are and what they mean. Nor, of course, could these unspecified limiteds be found to be in relation to equally unknown, unlimiteds. In addition Philolaus' *limiters* and *unlimiteds* are plural—and unknown—and that would make his cos-mological task as difficult as looking for a needle in a haystack. Finally, one must discount the notion that Philolaus was the first person to apply mathematical doctrines to philosophical problems, because his "philosophical problem" was to apply his musical scale to define the cosmos, and that great achievement had, as Heath pointed out, been accomplished by Pythagoras using precise science, mathematics and astronomy! In the case of Philolaus his having an interest in mathemat-ics, but not being mathematician, has much to do with his fanciful and unprovable system. In the end he appears as a dreamer, and perhaps his dream turned out merely to be an illusion.

In case there is still some controversy remaining as to whether Pythagoras or Philolaus is to be credited with the doctrines discussed (for the time being we omit those regarding Astronomy), it appears to me that the better course is not to rely on the speculations of phi-losophers and doxographers, but to give the highest honor to math-ematicians, scientists, and astronomers for whom such knowledge is their specialty. Therefore I defer to Sir Thomas Heath, whose books include *Aristarchus of Samos: The Ancient Copernicus,* and *A History of Greek Mathematics.* What is remarkable about these books is that despite being published in 1912 and 1921 respectively, they are still considered classics in their respective fields.

When we behold the remarkable list of scientific and mathematical achievements accorded to Pythagoras by a world-renowned mathematician and scientist such as Heath, they would seem to contradict Huffman's suggestion in A7a (by Plutarch) that it was Philolaus who originated the notion that "geometry was the mother-city of the mathematical sciences" (ibid., 107). Nor I think can we take seriously Huffman's inaccurate reference to A7a that Philolaus not only recognized a certain set of mathematical sciences—arithmetic, geometry, astronomy and music, but that "he even established a hierarchy of sciences with geometry as the basic science" (ibid., 54).

According to Heath, these achievements are to be credited to Pythagoras himself, and thus where Philolaus makes mention of these subjects we must assume—especially in light of the fact that he was "not primarily a mathematician"—that they are doctrines of Pythagoras to which Philolaus is referring. And where there are stark differences between the cosmologies of Pythagoras and Philolaus (notably with Pythagoras' transcendental Monad as source of the universe, which conflicts with Philolaus' claim that limited and unlimiteds—are plural, material origins of the universe) we must assume either that Philolaus abandoned other doctrines of Pythagoras in favor of his stated Presocratic beliefs, or that one hundred years after the birth of Pythagoras, his doctrines had become so changed, even distorted, that later philosophers, even including Aristotle, had no idea of the interpretation of the universe by Pythagoras himself.

One final point may be mentioned here. Many Western scholars have credited Philolaus for positing the idea that the musical intervals contained in the harmonia could be applied to our cosmos, but history shows, if we know where to look, that the discovery of the music of the spheres was so momentous a hypothesis, and so greatly misunderstood to this day, that it must undoubtedly be attributed to a great scientific genius, namely to Pythagoras himself.

And, not surprisingly, because having discovered the numerical (i.e., mathematical) relations between intervals in the octave, Pythagoras through long, painstaking and rigorous experiment, was also the first to *apply* this mathematical hypothesis to the planets in our solar system! Remarkably, he discovered that the distances between the planets were in correspondence with the numerical ratios of the diatonic scale, a hypothesis that incorporated the heliocentric theory, as has been confirmed by Sir Isaac Newton (see chapters "The Heliocentric Theory" and "Harmony of the Spheres"). Thus, two of the most profound discoveries in cosmology remain, to this day—without appropriate attribution—to Pythagoras. Even though Heath himself was among those who did not ascribe these discoveries to Pythagoras—so difficult were they to believe—he nevertheless described him as "one of the greatest names in the history of science."

As to Philolaus, the main reason why Philolaus' attempt to apply Pythagoras' diatonic scale, or harmonia, to the external world, indeed to the *structure* of the universe, can be considered nothing less than wishful thinking, is the following: Philolaus was not a mathematician. He did not *measure* the distances between the planets in our cosmos. He merely had an interest in mathematics and how mathematics could be applied to the external world.

As we have shown, prolonged and painstaking mathematical research was needed to understand the numerical relationships between musical intervals; and then to discover their mathematical application to the planetary system of our cosmos. The simple fact is that without having *exact mathematical proofs* of the *distances and relationships between the planets*, it would have been quite impossible for Philolaus to project a simple diatonic scale upon the cosmos and expect it to work. That task could only have been achieved by a scientific genius as great as Pythagoras!

When all is said and done, the *scriptures* reveal the source of our universe. That source is *Sound*. The first manifestation of the universe is found in sound. In the New Testament of The Christian Bible, the reference can be found in the Gospel of John 1:1: "In the beginning was the Word, and the Word was *with* God and the Word *was* God." In Hinduism, Buddhism, and other Eastern philosophies and religions, the sacred and primordial sound that includes and manifests the entire universe is "OM." The syllable *Om*, or *Aum*, which contains everything in the universe, is equivalent to Pythagoras' Monad, which also containes all things within its transcendental unity. Pythagoras knew this truth, and with his theory of the harmony of the spheres he demonstrates that a divine harmony of sound underlies the very structure of our universe.

CHAPTER 7

COSMOLOGY

I have pointed out that the Western philosophical tradition is weighted like a stone in favor of the Aristotelian perspective on reality, a perspective inherited by his pupil Theophrastus, and carried down the centuries by host of doxographers, who have influenced philosophers and historians—including Burkert, Huffman, Guthrie, Kahn, and many others—right up to our own time in the 21st century (see genealogical table on page 14).

It is now time for a metaphysician to provide a countervailing view to the Aristotelians regarding both Pythagoras and Philolaus. I begin by observing that most of the philosophers in the modern Aristotelian tradition have relied almost entirely upon their own discipline, namely philosophy, for answers to their questions. Few have ventured to explore the conclusions of mathematicians and astronomers, for whom cosmology is a specialty, and, judging by their pejorative conclusions over the years, few have explored other cultures or civilizations, ancient or modern.

The purpose of *our* investigation is to compare what we know of the cosmologies of Pythagoras and Philolaus. Indeed, some of the topics involving cosmology have been focused on in some measure in other chapters, for example on Number, as these issues are necessarily intertwined. Therefore I beg the indulgence of the reader for repeating the important aspects of those discussions as they apply to cosmology.

As we recall, Diogenes Laertius introduces Alexander Polyhistor, a philosopher and mathematician of the first century BC, by stating, "Alexander, in his book *Successions of Philosophers,* says he found in the *Pythagorean memoirs* the following tenets as well: 'The principle of all things is the monad, or unit; arising from this Monad the undefined dyad, or two, serves as material substratum to the Monad, which is cause'" (Laertius, 343).

From the viewpoint of metaphysicians, the first line, "the principle of all things is the Monad" is a transcendental statement regarding the origins of our universe. The Monad is the Absolute, God, or All That Is. It is also described as The Unit, not one unit among many, but The One and Only Unit. In fact, under the umbrella of All That Is, the Monad, as Unit, is also a unity. The transcendental unity of the Monad exists in its eternal effulgence before the manifestation of the universe begins—and, after the universe passes away, the transcendental Monad continues to exist, unchanged and eternal, and with the same divine effulgence.

The next two lines in Polyhistor are as follows: "Arising from this monad the undefined dyad or two, serves as material substratum to the monad, which is cause." There are important cosmological statements embedded here. The first is that the Monad is the cause of *all* existence. The next is that from this Monad *arises* a second principle, described as two. This second principle is termed an "undefined dyad" and, to simplify, although also divine and eternal, the Monad has limited part of itself to embody the entire universe. It is therefore *considered* a material principle that *arises* from its transcendental Source, and serves as substratum to the Monad.

As with Hinduism and Buddhism the single principle, the Monad, flows outward into existence and creates, or *emanates* into, the world of Nature. And Nature, our cosmos, here described as a material substratum, is essentially a material projection of the Monad into matter.

Insofar as number is concerned, the Pythagorean Monad is described as the Unit, One; and the undefined dyad, which serves as the material substratum, is defined as two. Because these statements echo and mirror sophisticated cosmologies from Hinduism and Buddhism, I take them to have come from Pythagoras himself, and not to a student or follower who fell under the label of "the Pythagoreans." Let us be quite clear that with the cosmic emanation of the Monad into the undefined dyad, the realm of duality is born. The world of duality is created in that cosmic "moment" of expression that heralds a new cosmic cycle of existence is about to begin. The world of duality is born simultaneously with the emanation, or the differentiation of the Monad, into its material body, the undefined dyad.

In addition, we must take particular note of the term "dyad" attributed to Nature as the material aspect of the Monad. A dyad is comprised of two things, in this case the eternal Monad, and the "undefined dyad," but the term *dyad* implies, that the originating principles are ever part of one cosmic energy (as the Hindu cosmology confirms). What this means is that the Monad *is also* the undefined dyad. What many scientists cannot see or will not accept is that the divine energy of the Monad permeates every particle of our material cosmos as assuredly as it reigns supreme in its own eternal realm. The world of duality is merely confirmation of the spontaneous explosion of the divine Monad into the entire cosmos.

I note that for the Eastern world, the Hindus and Buddhists, there is no such thing as the Western, scientific, Big Bang, where something explodes into existence out of nothing, and with no attributable source. From time immemorial the East has held a quite different explanation of our origins. For the Eastern world, as with Pythagoras, the Monad exists eternally, and at the moment of cosmic law heralding its new cycle of existence, it begins first by emanating itself into the indefinite dyad then, by stages, into the entire cosmos. It is a cosmic cycle endlessly repeating itself, taking eons of time to accomplish. When the entire cosmic cycle is completed, the Monad, and the universe, fold back into their eternal source, where they remain in an unmanifested form until the "moment" when the next cycle of manifestation will begin. This is the simple metaphysical explanation of our universe.

The first expressions of the world of duality as it applies to Earth are time and space. However, all the other dualities are born at the same time. A list of the opposites, described as doctrines of the Pythagoreans, is provided by Aristotle in *Metaphysics* (I 5 986 a 23), but they are repeated for convenience on page 78.

I have several objections to the way the list has been interpreted; but I will set them aside until the end of this short exposition. In my book on Plato, I suggested that there should be two more opposites: eternity-temporality and life–death. One notes, too, that Aristotle heads the list

limited	unlimited
odd	even
one	plurality
right	left
male	female
at rest	moving
straight	crooked
light	darkness
good	bad
square	oblong

with *Limit* and *Unlimited,* terms we have come to associate with the cosmogony of Philolaus.

My objection to the list of opposites is that, to a metaphysician such as Pythagoras, they do not make any sense. For example, the terms One and Plurality should head the list, as the One refers to the Monad, and the Plurality refers to the undefined dyad, or Nature, and the "ten thousand things" of our mundane, material existence.

The terms *Limit* and *Unlimited* have also been incorrectly designated. From a metaphysical standpoint *Unlimited* refers to the Monad, and *Limited* refers to the things in this world that exist under the rubric of the undefined dyad, or Nature. In addition, the Monad, described as the Unlimited cannot be limited by anything other than Itself. Under Aristotle's system, the Monad should be called Odd. Why? Because the Monad is One, it is singular and eternal. Therefore it cannot be Even. The term Even which Aristotle equates with unlimited, is not true in metaphysical terms, because Even designates that which is limited— i.e., the world of Nature, not the Unlimited. (This is perhaps what Plato had in mind in the *Philebus* when he says that one has a share of the One and the many, the limited and unlimited in them.) One should note, in addition, that the "chaos" some philosophers have contended exists before the world is born is a speculation dreamed up by people to describe the unknown. However, the "chaos" does not exist. Our universe, as Plato revealed, is a copy of the eternal world in material form. There is no "chaos" in God.

Considering the importance of Even and Odd in Aristotle's version of the Pythagorean system, his misinterpretation of the cosmic expression of these terms turns the metaphysical world upside down, and substitutes a list of confused, illogical, misunderstood designations of things. And, one might note, some of the pairs in the list of opposites are things one can perceive and experience in the material world; while other pairs, such as One/plurality and good/bad are terms that derive from what Plato would refer to as the intelligible world. Thus the authority of Aristotle on the matter of the opposites is found to be quite unreliable.

Aristotle's own bafflement and misunderstanding of Pythagorean doctrines is well documented in his own works (*Metaphysics, De Caelo, Physics*). Therefore *we* must take particular care that we do not allow his misinterpretation to misconstrue *our* metaphysical principles—as, sadly, he has managed to do over the last two thousand years. And if it is true that his misinterpretations rest upon the doctrines of Philolaus, then one has only to consult the template by Alexander Polyhistor to confirm that the doctrines of Philolaus have nothing at all in common with what I contend to be the true philosophy of Pythagoras represented in that document.

To return to Polyhistor's "template," it is remarkable that the first two lines contain the entire cosmogony of Pythagoras in a most succinct and crystallized form. The template continues as follows:

> From the monad and the undefined dyad spring numbers; from numbers, points; from points, lines; from lines, plane figures; from plane figures, solid figures; from solid figures, sensible bodies, the elements of which are four, fire, water, earth and air; these elements interchange and turn into one another. (Laertius, 343).

Note: The Platonic solids are an integral part of this unfolding. Indeed, they represent the archetypal patterns of the four elements: earth, water, fire, and air, each of which is a different geometric shape and a correspondingly different number of faces and allotted a different function in the world of Nature (see diagram, page 108).

Again, remarkably, Pythagoras explains the gradual emanation of the Monad into matter—a journey encompassing endless eons of time—into the space of a few simple lines of crystallized wisdom. However, one would need to descend almost to the bottom of the cosmic "floor" to arrive at the four elements that the Presocratic scientist/philosophers, including Philolaus, took to be the *material* origin of our world. Plato shows us that even the elements have a divine origin.

As we focus upon Philolaus, let us recall that Diogenes Laertius had stated: "There are some who insist, absurdly enough, that Pythagoras left no writings whatever" (Laertius, 5). "Pythagoras, in fact, wrote three books: *On Education; On Statemanship;* and *On Nature.* But the book that passes as the work of Pythagoras is by Lysis of Tarentum, a Pythagorean who fled to Thebes and taught Epaminondas." Of course there is no proof that the book that "passed as the work of Pythagoras" was by Lysis. But it is certainly a strange coincidence that the book *On Nature,* attributed to Philolaus, should have the very same title as the book *On Nature* attributed to Pythagoras.

Huffman opens the chapter on cosmogony by saying, "The primary sources for Philolaus' cosmogony are seemingly meager indeed [fr. 17], about six lines in total, but they are absolutely crucial for understanding Philolaus' philosophy and for evaluating Aristotle's accounts of Pythagoreanism" (Huffman, 203).

Fragment 1 of Philolaus book, *On Nature,* represents his "central thesis." (Parenthetically I note that this fragment appears under the section Basic Principles, not under the section entitled, Philolaus' Philosophy, which is where I would have expected it to appear.) There are other such peculiar placements of fragments in Huffman's book. For example, there are *no texts* by Philolaus in the chapter on Astronomy, only "texts *relevant* to the astronomical system of Philolaus." As Huffman also reveals: The only fragments which are relevant to the astronomical system are fragments 7 and 17, which I have already discussed (ibid., 241–242). However, let us review:

Fragment 1: "Nature in the world order was fitted together both out of things which are unlimited and things which are limiting, both the world order and everything in it" (ibid., 37).

Since Philolaus is taken by the majority of the Western philosophical tradition to have been a student of Pythagoras, a follower, or a possible successor (albeit at least one hundred years later) and as the *first* of *the Pythagoreans* to have published a book, what Philoaus says must be closely followed. History depends upon it.

The first thing one notices is that Philolaus is focusing on Nature as the origin of our cosmos, a position that is diametrically opposed to Pythagoras' transcendental term of origin, the Monad, or God. Nature is the term that we use to describe the physical world around us, a world first interpreted by our senses. Huffman often counts Philolaus as a Presocratic, one of the Ionian scientist-philosophers who sought the origin of our world in the natural elements. As Patricia Curd reminds us in her valuable book *A Presocratics Reader: Selected Fragments and Testimonia*: "In rejecting divine authority for their claims, the Presocratics invite inquiry into the sources of human knowledge" (Curd, 5). Clearly Pythagoras' Monad and Philolaus' Nature are diametrically opposed interpretations. Philolaus has said that Nature in the world order was fitted together by both unlimited things and limiting things. In fact, for Philolaus, the world order is composed of two opposing, undefined, groups of things, groups of things that are unlimited and groups of things that are limited. For Pythagoras, the origin of existence, the Monad, God, is divine; it is One and it is a unity. Here is revealed the second fissure in their worldviews.

Here are a few statements meant to help clarify Philolaus' position. "Limiters and unlimiteds are not treated as abstract principles divorced from the world, but rather manifest features of the world" (Huffman, 40). Philolaus assumes that the world has "to arise from origins that are plural" (ibid., 50), and it seems he relied "on direct appeal to sense experience to establish the existence of limiters and unlimiteds" (ibid., 66).

Surprisingly, Huffman explains that Philolaus did not tell us what he meant by limiters and unlimiteds, nor did he provide a single example of them in the fragments (ibid., 37). He argues, however, that limiters and unlimiteds are a natural development out of Presocratic thought, but that Philolaus went further because limiters and unlimiteds differ from Presocratic principles in that they are not determined by any quantity (water, air, etc.), but rather mark out a continuum of possible quantities.

In fact, Huffman asserts that Philolaus had introduced a "distinct class of unlimited (namely time, void, and musical pitch) that is probably and indirectly based upon the introduction of limiters, along with unlimiteds, as basic constituents of reality" (ibid., 51) and, furthermore, that these unlimiteds "actually constitute part of the structure of our world." Huffman adds that, if *we* could find explicit examples of things that are "fitted together," we ought to be able to identify "what is limiting and what is unlimited in such a compound" (ibid., 41). Such an example, he suggests, is found in:

> Fragment 7: "The first thing fitted together the one in the center of the sphere, is called the hearth."

Huffman equates the hearth with the "central fire" and the "central fire" as unlimited—"and the middle of the sphere [because it] determines the fire's position spatially, at the center, as a limiter." For more examples of unlimiteds (but with an incorrect interpretation), Huffman relies on Aristotle.

> Fragment 201: "The universe is one and it drew from the unlimited time, breath, and void, which in each case distinguishes the place of each thing."

Huffman finds the most interesting and original example of the relation of limiters and unlimiteds is found in music. On a monochord, "the string and the indefinite number of pitches it can produce can be compared to the unlimited, while stops placed along it to determine specific pitches are the limiters" (ibid., 44). One might quibble here with Huffman, who omits Aristotle's term, breath, and substitutes for it the term musical pitch. What is more concerning, as we have shown elsewhere, is that Philolaus, or, indeed, Huffman, turns Aristotle's group of limiteds—time, breath, and void—into a series of unlimiteds that would supposedly align with Philolaus' interpretation of them. As Huffman says: "...the passage of Aristotle is as close as we get to a series of examples of what Philolaus meant by unlimiteds" (ibid., 44).

Reviewing the quotation by Aristotle, it is hard to understand Huffman's insistence on designating them as Philolaus' unlimiteds when Aristotle clearly stated that the universe drew from the unlimited time, breath, and void, and thus meant them to stand as limiters. In fact, there appears to be a contradiction in Philolaus as to what constitutes the original "principles" of cosmology. Huffman has been arguing all along that limiters and unlimiteds claim the place of honor in the system of Philolaus, but fragment 7, above, states, "The *first* thing fitted together, the one in the center of the *sphere* is called the hearth." It is a surprising turn of events, because having established limiters and unlimiteds as his basic principles, which arose from Nature, and stating that Philolaus never said what he meant by limiters and unlimiteds, nor gave a single example of them, he is at the same time claiming that the *first* thing fitted together, the one in the center of the *sphere*, is called the hearth.

These are quite specific designations that appear to supplant limiters and unlimiteds as originating principles. Clearly, a sphere is already present, and in the center of it—as the first thing fitted together—is the hearth, which is clarified later to be the central fire. From where did these concepts suddenly appear, fully grown, as it were? That is a mystery one wishes Philolaus would have unraveled. Instead, he takes us further into the mystery by claiming that the Earth is no longer to be considered the center of our universe, and that it must be displaced in favor of the "central fire."

As I have explained elsewhere, the central fire is a new term of origin for Philolaus—as a Presocratic. He has taken the old Presocratic, quantitative appellation of the four elements as originating principles, and extrapolated from them fire as origin, and moved it upward (into his continuum of unlimiteds) to become the central fire—a fire that has now evolved into an *invisible* concept of fire. Let us be clear, the central fire, or hearth, as originating principle has nothing in common with the divine Monad of Pythagoras, and it also violates Philolaus' own Presocratic roots because it is no longer a natural element. In fact it makes me wonder whether Philolaus had not patterned his "central fire" upon Pythagoras' Sun at the center of the cosmos in the heliocentric theory, to which I believe Philolaus was privy. Where else would a non-mathematician come up with a paradigm-changing theory that displaces Earth from the center of the cosmos? We leave aside the fact that the sphere was already present before the central fire, as hearth, was fitted together to arrive at its central place of honor. That is another mystery we wish Philolaus (or Huffman) had unraveled for us.

The earth-shaking fact in the midst of this cosmic picture is that the Earth has been displaced from its place at the center of our universe. To reiterate: how is it that someone who could not define his original principles of limit and unlimited, and who then asks us to believe that an invisible central fire is the hearth of the universe, now charge us to believe that he originated the idea that the Earth should be displaced from its center? I would reiterate: Here the impression prevails that Philolaus had somehow come to be exposed to some of the secret teachings of Pythagoras, albeit one hundred years later, and he either does not understand the teachings metaphysically, or he chose to reinterpret them with a Presocratic cast of mind. Either way, his cosmology has nothing in common with Pythagoras, and yet many accept him as Pythagoras' "successor." It required a genius of the highest order to have arrived at the notion of displacing the Earth from the center of the cosmos, and replacing it not with Philolaus' central fire, but with our Sun! Pythagoras' remarkable hypothesis was achieved by painstaking scientific, mathematical and astronomical research which provided sound evidence that was rediscovered and confirmed by Sir Isaac Newton two thousand years later. Philolaus here shows himself, once again, to be the Presocratic follower in the steps of the divine Master, Pythagoras.

However, in the section "Basic Principles," Huffmann also includes a fragment attributed to Stobaeus:

> Fragment 6 "Concerning nature and harmony the situation is this: The being of things, which is eternal, and nature in itself admit of divine and not human knowledge, except that it was impossible for any of the things that are and are known by us to have come to be, if the being of the things from which the world-order came together, both the limiting things and the unlimited things, did not preexist." (Huffman, 123–124)

Huffman, wearing his Presocratic hat, interprets the above fragment as meaning that the being of limiters and unlimiteds must have preexisted. But a metaphysician would interpret that passage differently. If one places dashes in between being-of-things and nature-in-itself, the passage reads: "Concerning nature and harmony, the being-of-things (Monad) which is eternal, and nature-in-itself (undefined dyad) admit of divine and not human knowledge, except that it was impossible for any of the things that are and are known by us (which includes both limiting things and unlimited things)...to have come to be, *if the being-of-things, from which the world order came together did not preexist."*

On this view, the metaphysical view, God, the Monad, the Source is divine. Nothing can exist in the material world other than having been created by God, because God preexists even the conception of the material realm, as the Alexander Polyhistor template confirms. This latter, metaphysical view is that of Pythagoras.

Finally, let us view the only other cosmological fragment, from the *Bacchae* of Philolaus:

Fragment 17: "The world order is one. It began to come to be right up at the middle and from the middle [came to be] upward in the same way as downward and the things above the middle are symmetrical with those below. For, in the lower [regions] the lowest part [for the upper regions] is like the highest and similarly for the rest. For both [the higher and the lower] have the same relationship to the middle, except that their positions are reversed" (ibid., 215).

Apart from impressions of a vague similarity with the baffling mystery in Plato's tale of the origin of our world in the *Timaeus*, there is not much that communicates itself to us of the world order, except that its parts are symmetrical to one another.

One phrase, however, cannot escape our notice: it is important, because in this case Philolaus himself is given attribution for the quotation. It is the opening phrase: "The world order *is one."* This phrase, once again, is in direct contradiction to his claim that limiters and unlimiteds were plural originating, material principles, and that the world-order could not be established without a harmonia supervening upon them. As Philolaus had stated, some of these unlimiteds and limiters were in harmony with the world order, and needed no harmonia. Only those which were unlike were in need of the harmonia.

Just as it is an impossible claim to suggest that limiters and unlimiteds are originating, plural, material principles and at the same time to claim that the central fire, or hearth is the first thing "fitted together," it is equally impossible to suggest that the world-order is one, and at the same time claim that at least *some* limiters and unlimiteds are not part of the world order—at least not until *pleasing intervals* of the harmonia, bring them into it.

As we have discussed under the chapter on Harmonia, Pythagoras discovered the numerical intervals and the octave, which comprise the remarkably simple beginnings of Western music. Howard Goodall, the renowned musicologist describes music as "one of the dazzling fruits of Western civilization," and we might note that those same numerical intervals were later shown to be in symmetrical correspondence with all the planets in our solar system.

Philolaus doubtless was aware of Pythagoras' diatonic scale, and believed he could apply it to his own cosmological hypothesis with the central fire at the center of a world consisting of plural/material limiters and unlimiteds. But Philolaus' effort was doomed to failure for two reasons: the first is that the central fire was an *invisible* element; it thus had no precise location in the center of the cosmos, and therefore no ratios or relations of *any* planets could be attributed to it. Second, he lacked the incredible genius of Pythagoras in *mathematically determining* the exact distances of the planets—from the Sun—and not the Earth! We may agree that there are elements of Pythagorean thought in Philolaus' work, but in the end those doctrines are applied by Philolaus to ends that are clearly Presocratic. In fact, they have severely damaged the reputation of the Pythagoreans, because so many scholars down the ages have bought into the idea that Philolaus was himself a Pythagorean, even, possibly the successor to Pythagoras. When we compare the cosmology of Pythagoras with that of Philolaus we find two diametrically opposed sets of doctrines of which it seems, no harmonia could possibly find pleasing correspondences.

♷

As Huffman presciently observes, "Most of the rest of his (Philolaus') astronomical system can be seen as trying to square the obvious phenomena with this initial postulate" (ibid., 244)—namely, the central fire.

CHAPTER 8

THE HELIOCENTRIC THEORY

The heliocentric theory, discovered by Pythagoras, has inspired controversy and outright disbelief throughout the ages. That is understandable when, in the ancient world, scientific theories of the universe, the planetary system, and the placement of the planets were still in relative infancy. Sir Thomas Heath places Pythagoras, in the ancient world as follows:

> In a former chapter we tried to differentiate from the astronomical system of "the Pythagoreans" the views put forward by the Master himself, and we saw reason for believing that he was the first to give spherical shape to the Earth and the heavenly bodies generally, and to assign to the planets a revolution of their own in a sense opposite to that of the daily rotation of the sphere of the fixed stars about the Earth as center. (Heath, *Aristarchus of Samos*, 93)

Heath continues:

> But a much more remarkable development was to follow in the Pythagorean school. This was nothing less than the abandonment of the geocentric hypothesis, and the reduction of the Earth to the status of a planet like the others. Aetius [probably on the authority of Theophrastus] attributes the resulting system to Philolaus; Aristotle [attributes it] to "the Pythagoreans." (ibid.)

Note that the doxographer, Aetius attributes the system to Philolaus, but Theophrastus, successor of Aristotle in the Lyceum, is assumed to be speaking for Aristotle, when he attributes the system to the Pythagoreans (but not Philolaus himself.) Here we find represented a familiar difference between the doctrines of Philolaus, and the historically later

Aristotelian view of the cosmos, which rejects the notion of the central fire, and continues in the ancient belief that the Earth was the center of the cosmos.

As for Pythagoras, after all the many ground breaking achievements that Heath has attributed to him in his book *Aristarchus of Samos: The Ancient Copernican,* including the inauguration of geometry as a science and the discovery of the theory of numbers and *means,* all crucial in determining astronomical proofs, Heath states:

> It is improbable that Pythagoras was responsible for the astro-nomical system known as Pythagorean, in which the Earth was deposed from its place at rest in the centre of the universe, and became a 'planet' like the Sun and Moon and the other planets revolving about the central fire. *For Pythagoras the Earth was still at the center.* (ibid., 163)

There is little doubt that in the ancient world an earth-shaking revo-lution occurred in cosmology, and most philosophers take it for granted that it was initiated by Philolaus. In fact, his system is described as the *Pythagorea*n system. We must bear in mind, however, that the system of Philolaus bears absolutely no correlation to the document revealed by Alexander Polyhistor, which I have used as a template for outlin-ing the cosmological doctrines of Pythagoras. In the preface to that document it is claimed that the tenets included therein came from the memoirs of Pythagoras. This in itself should give us pause.

In addition I would point out that the introduction of the central fire that was to depose the Earth from the center of the cosmos was not a Pythagorean doctrine, but a quasi-Presocratic notion which merely substituted for one element, earth, another "element," the central fire, to take the place of honor as center of the cosmos. Here Philolaus clearly has in mind the Presocratic focus on the elements as originating principles of our world. However, Philolaus' new interpretation of the cosmos also violates the Presocratic dictum that sought for the origin of the world in the natural elements water, air, earth, or fire. Nor does it appear to include limiters and unlimiteds. The central fire that Phi-lolaus now envisages at the center of the solar system is not the natural element of fire, but an *invisible* concept of fire around which revolve all of the "scientifically" designated planets, as well as the Sun, Moon, and fixed stars. There is no trace of Pythagoras in this fanciful notion! The central fire is not a Pythagorean notion; at best it can be designated as a quasi-Presocratic doctrine. And yet, practically all the scholars of the Western philosophical tradition are content to attribute it, unquestioningly, to "the Pythagorean school."

The complete inability of Philolaus to describe or scientifically designate the central fire or the counter-earth amounts to a tragic miscarriage of justice in that these fanciful and totally unprovable doctrines have been laid, over the centuries, at the feet of the Pythagoreans. In fact, irreparable damage has been done to the reputation of the Pythagoreans due to the ill-fated belief by scholars that the system of Philolaus is Pythagorean when nothing could be further from the truth.

It seems Aristotle may have been aware of this dissonance between Philolaus and the Pythagoreans when he did not attribute the new planetary system to Philolaus. However, the knowledge that Aristotle inherited about Philolaus and the Pythagoreans, as well as his own scientific worldview, caused him to make the same mistake, namely to accuse the Pythagoreans of having a fanciful and unscientific astronomical system.

Merely comparing Aristotle's astronomical system with that of Philolaus, admittedly of one hundred years later, shows how many planetary blanks in Philolaus' system have been filled in, and shows the Earth again at the center of the cosmos (see diagrams, page 90). Nonetheless, Aristotle's interpretation of the Pythagorean cosmos is colored by Philolaus' doctrines as well as his own prejudices against the Pythagoreans. As is well documented, he was baffled by and misunderstood Pythagorean mathematics, their doctrine of essences and substances, and their metaphysical theories; he believed that, although the Pythagoreans dealt in abstract concepts, they applied their theories to the "sensibles" of the material world.

When one considers that the towering figure of Aristotle has cast his shadow over Western science and philosophy for the last two thousand years, some blame must be laid at his door for the persistent mockery and/or rejection of Pythagorean doctrines that he did not understand. Rejection that has persisted in the ideas of his innumerable followers to the present day.

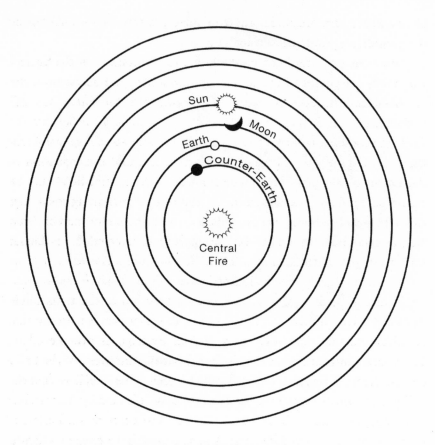

Philolaus' planetary system

In hindsight, this displacement of the Earth at the center of the cosmos for the central fire, appears to be a step backward in scientific understanding of our world. And, although most modern scholars continue to interpret Philolaus as though, in his own time, he was a serious contender in moving the evolution of the cosmos forward, we do see in Aristotle a rejection of that theory in his diagram of the cosmos, which installs Earth once again at the center (see diagram, page 92).

Let us now shift our attention to Pythagoras. It is true that Heath's books on Greek cosmology and mathematics are timeless classics in their field. In fact they thankfully go beyond the vague speculations and fanciful thinking of much of the Presocratic world, and show us scientific and mathematical *proofs* about the cosmos that many philosophers have misunderstood or merely dismissed—as shown by the prejudice against the Pythagoreans.

However, one area that Heath failed to understand in the ancient world was the genius of Pythagoras in discovering the heliocentric theory. As Heath mistakenly claims "For Pythagoras the *Earth* was still at the center" (ibid., 163). In fact so certain was he in his belief that the Pythagorean *school*—and not Pythagoras himself—was responsible for the "abandonment of the geocentric hypotheses and the reduction of the Earth to the status of a planet...circling the central fire," that he assumes, seemingly without question, that this earth-shaking cosmological event was engineered by Philolaus, a man of whom Huffman had said "he was not a mathematician" but had "plenty of interest" in mathematics! In this particular case Heath was clearly wrong. As we shall show, *Pythagoras* discovered the heliocentric theory—*in the sixth century* BC.

Considering the towering genius evident in all of the remarkable discoveries Heath records of Pythagoras in his books, it is ironic that Heath's own intuition failed to side with Pythagoras over Philolaus. The widespread confusion to this day about the discovery of the heliocentric theory is revealed in the fact that Heath came to believe that the heliocentric theory was first put forward and defended by Aristarchus of Samos, an ancient Copernican, in the third century BC. Philolaus' displacement of Earth for the central fire must have created a world-shaking controversy at the time. And those with a more superficial understanding of cosmology may have wrongly concluded that what Philolaus was advocating was a *heliocentric* theory, one placing the *Sun* at the center of the solar system. When one considers that Philolaus was deemed by some a "successor," a descendant, or as Huffman says, even a "follower" of Pythagoras—one hundred years later—it does make one wonder anew whether he had heard of Pythagoras' heliocentric theory, and adapted it to his own purposes.

In fact, *rumors* of a heliocentric theory, attributable to the Pythagoreans, floated about as late as the time of Aristotle, who remarked on it, and soundly rejected the theory. Philolaus' own theory placing the central fire at the center of the cosmos instead of the Sun, must have added much to the confusion. The world now knows that Nicholas Copernicus (1473–1543), a Polish astronomer and mathematician

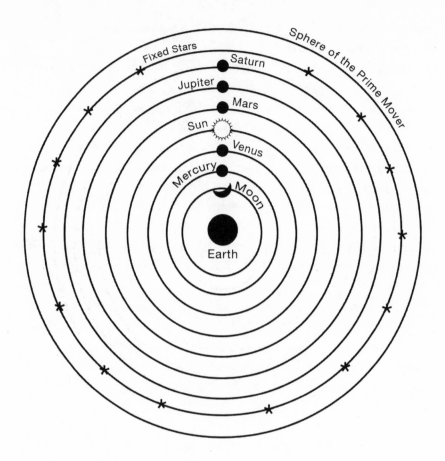

Geocentric Universe of Aristotle and Ptolemy

of the sixteenth century, presented (we would say "rediscovered") the heliocentric hypothesis. It was an earthshaking event both astronomically and in human consciousness.

In fact, the reputations of four of the greatest scientists and astronomers in history are embedded in the heliocentric theory—Copernicus, Galileo, Kepler, and Newton. What was their connection to sixth-century-BC Pythagoras and/or Philolaus and the Pythagoreans? As a prelude to that remarkable discovery of the heliocentric hypothesis, a very brief account of its historical "evolution" would give a useful context.

In the fourth century BC a theory prevailed, attributed to Heraclides of Pontus, that the "planets (Mercury and Venus) revolved in circles about the Sun as center, while the Sun revolved in a larger circle

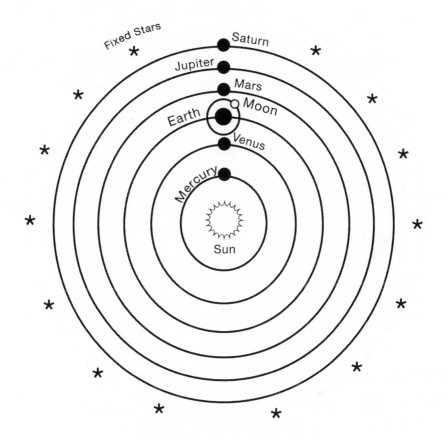

Copernicus' planetary system

about the Earth" (Armitage, 29): "The limited heliocentric system was extended to include Mars, Jupiter, and Saturn, so *that all five planets would thus be supposed to revolve about the Sun while the Sun revolved about the Earth.*" He adds,

> This would have marked an important step toward the Copernican scheme; and, early in the third century BC, Aristarchus of Samos actually anticipated the full Copernican system in its broad outlines.... The hypotheses of Aristarchus, however, were generally rejected as impious and contrary to sound physical principles. Moreover, such undeveloped speculations had soon to compete with the carefully articulated systems of the Alexandrine astronomers, which represented inequities in the

apparent motions of the Sun and planets with steadily increasing numerical accuracy. These systems were conceived on the geocentric hypothesis and their success did much to establish it.... To encapsulate, the theories of planetary motion became obscure, and gradually evolved into two different systems, one dealing with movable eccentrics and the other into a complicated system of epicycles. (Armitage, 29–32)

Moving ahead:

Ptolemy's lunar and planetary theory completed the achievements of Greek and Alexandrian astronomy, the roots of which lay deep in the ancient civilization of the East. He wrought the whole into the comprehensive, logical system of astronomy set forth in a treatise now commonly known as the *Almagest*. The authority of this work [completed about AD 145] was solidly on the side of the geocentric theory, and it dominated all the developments of astronomy...until the sixteenth century, when the book served as a quarry from which Copernicus extracted many of the data and geometrical methods he employed in his efforts to *subvert* that authority. (ibid., 36–37)

Armitage explains that "in the fifteenth century there occurred a remarkable revival of astronomical studies...stimulated by the recovery of the classics of ancient science and philosophy in their original Greek instead of corrupted translations...and aided by the invention of printing. With the widening of the literary horizon, opinions which Aristotle had ignored or flouted, now came again to be discussed—the theories of Philolaus, of Heraclides, of Aristarchus...all tending to bring the geocentric theory into dispute."

In a section 6, "Precursors of Copernicus," Armitage begins with an extract from the *De placiti philosophorum* of pseudo-Plutarch: "It is commonly maintained that the Earth is at rest. But Philolaus the Pythagorean held that it revolved round the Fire in an oblique circle in like manner to the Sun and Moon" (ibid., 87). As precursors Armitage also includes Heraclides of Pontus, Ecphantus the Pythagorean, Aristarchus of Samos, Cicero's account of Hicetas, and Martianus Capella. I beg the indulgence of the reader for this brief overview, but for a full, eminently readable account of the evolution of planetary theories from the ancient world up to the time of Copernicus, I heartily recommend Angus Armitage's book *Copernicus: The Founder of Modern Astronomy.*

Armitage mentions Pythagoras early in his book. He enumerates his many scientific, mathematical, and astronomical achievements. He tells us Pythagoras was aware of two simple motions of the Sun: a) the motion of the heavenly bodies whereby they appear to revolve about an axis through the Earth once in a day; and b) the motion of the Sun in a direction contrary to the first motion, and taking place about a different axis, in the space of one year.

> The first of these motions would account for the daily rising and setting of the Sun; the second would account for the Sun's annual circuit among the constellations and for the seasonal fluctuations in its rising and setting points and in its meridian altitude. This analysis seems also to have been extended by Pythagoras (although with less eligibility) to the apparent motion of the Moon and planets; it gave rise to the idea that the complicated movements of the heavenly bodies could all be resolved into *uniform circular motions.* This doctrine was established by the authority of Plato, Aristotle, and Ptolemy: as we see it still dominated astronomy in the time of Copernicus, two thousand years after Pythagoras, and it was first formally abandoned by Kepler [for elliptical planetary orbits] at the beginning of the seventeenth century. (ibid., 23–24)

So well has Pythagoras concealed his own achievement regarding the discovery of the heliocentric theory that Armitage reports:

> By the end of the fifth century BC, the Pythagorean school had evolved the remarkable system of cosmology associated with the name of Philolaus. To this hypothesis Copernicus directed especial attention, for it was the earliest system to displace the Earth from the center of the universe and set it in revolution about the center [ed. the central fire] like any other planet (ibid., 24).

After giving details of Philolaus' planetary system, Armitage concludes: "The somewhat fanciful system of Philolaus never established itself; but the primitive Pythagorean cosmology lived on in the natural philosophy of Plato...especially in the *Timaeus* and the *Republic*" (ibid., 25).

COPERNICUS

The purpose of introducing the great physicists of the sixteenth and seventeenth centuries is with the single intention of finding connections between their discoveries and known doctrines of Pythagoras. In the case of Copernicus, these connections are foundational. When Copernicus surveyed the Western planetary theories, especially those of Plato, Aristotle, and Ptolemy he found among them strong support for the geocentric theory. Later on, rival theories, which had developed from the eccentrics and epicycles of the Alexandrine astronomers, yielded tables of practical value; but they admitted much that was contrary to sound physics. In his disappointment Copernicus turned to the ancient philosophers to see what alternative theories they might have proposed.

He found references that Hicetas, Philolaus, Aristarchus, and others had suggested a belief in the motion of the Earth, and this knowledge provided inspiration for his own research that ultimately culminated in the heliocentric hypothesis. Armitage ponders "whether Copernicus really derived his inspiration from these classic passages or whether he merely quoted them" (ibid., 71). In the case of Philolaus, since Armitage reminds us that his planetary theory, in the end, was discarded as fanciful, it is unlikely that it contributed in any further way to Copernicus' scientific and mathematical breakthrough into the heliocentric hypothesis. I would suggest that Copernicus found in these authors *references* to the Earth in motion, but that they provided the *inspiration* to seek answers for himself—answers that would reverberate in the sixteenth and seventeenth centuries. He was amply rewarded for his unorthodox plan.

The doctrine current in his time was that the motions of the heavenly bodies could all be resolved into uniform, eternal and *circular* motion—a doctrine established by the authority of Plato, Aristotle, and Ptolemy. In chapter 4 of Copernicus' book *De Revolutionibus,* he affirms that the bodies are uniform, eternal, and circular. But, having examined Hicetas, Philolaus, and Aristarchus he began to wonder whether the *Earth* is also motionless, as classical doctrine decreed, or whether it moved—and whether a planet as tiny as Earth in the center of the universe could support the whole planetary system revolving around it. In short Copernicus accepted Aristotle and Ptolemy's laws of circular planetary motion, but he began to challenge their declaration that the Earth was at rest. He therefore challenged the notion that the rectilinear movement of the elements air, water, fire, earth, was toward the *center of the universe*, and gave the same explanation regarding heavy bodies. He also challenged the notion that if the Earth performed its daily rotation, it would throw all bodies off into space rather than draw them, by "gravitation" to its center. Copernicus rejected these classical theories and he posited that each body—terrestrial and celestial—possessed a natural *circular* motion.

He summed up his findings on the heliocentric hypothesis as follows. The summary of his book states: "The characteristic apparent motions of the planets, with their stationary points and arcs of retrogression...can be simply accounted for, once for all, as optical effects resulting from the orbital revolution of the terrestrial observer round *the Sun*" (ibid., 90).

Although it turned out that Copernicus' mechanical model was no more accurate than Aristotle or Ptolemy, in that it retained their decree that the planetary orbits were still *circular*, it did establish that the center of the universe is the Sun and it did determine the relative distances of planets from the Sun. The substitution of the heliocentric hypothesis also simplified greatly the construction of tables for computing a planet's position in the sky at any given time (ibid., 93).

Armitage concludes by saying that the great contribution of Copernicus to astronomy lay "in his development of those ideas into a systematic planetary theory, capable of furnishing tables of an accuracy not before attained, and embodying a principle, the adoption of which was to make possible the triumphs of Kepler and Newton in the following century.

GALILEO

The opening words of the preface to Galileo's book *Dialogue on World Systems*, reads as follows: "There was published some years since a salutiferous edict, which for the obviating of the dangerous Scandals of the present Age, imposed *a seasonable Silence upon the Pythagorean Opinion of the Mobility of the Earth*" (de Santillana, *Reflections*, 190). Presumably a similar silence prevailed in the time of Santillana (1902–1974), because the title of his essay, "Philolaus in Limbo, or What Happened to the Pythagoreans?" was included in his book *Reflections on Men and Ideas*. Santillana's article goes on to name various scholars who have misjudged the history of the Pythagoreans, focusing mainly on Eric Frank, and he tells us:

> The invisible edict, or "trend," to which we refer has decreed that the whole development of Greek mathematics and astronomy be condensed into a rather short interval of time around 400 BC so that almost all the mathematics, astronomy, and music theory of the "so-called Pythagoreans" becomes contemporary with Plato and his successors. (ibid., 190)

Santillana then lists several schools that

> find this viewpoint particularly congenial. One is the massed power of Platonic and Aristotelian scholarship...a second one is a school of hypercritical philologists starting with Eva Sachs and continuing through Erik Frank's *Plato und die Sogenannten Pythagoreer* (1923) and a third is the recent school of scientific historians which has attempted to trace the connection between Babylonian and Greek mathematics. Of their work we may cite the papers of O. Neugebauer, K. Reidmeister, and B. L. van der Waerden. Relying on Frank, these authors have dismissed the entire tradition about early Greek mathematics, and supplanted it either with a most improbably late transference of Babylonian mathematics to Greece in the fifth century, or else have tried to fill the gap with speculations, conceived certainly by conjectural traces in Euclid and Plato. Frank's general thesis is this: There is no Greek science in any real sense before Anaxagoras and Democritus. (ibid., 190–191)

It did not help Pythagoras, of course, that his critical doctrines were secret and restricted to immediate acolytes, but it is ironic that despite's Aristotle telling us that above all the Pythagoreans sought mathematical proofs for their theories, the historical image that remains is that of Philolaus, with his fanciful and mathematically unproven speculations being taken for an authentic Pythagorean.

As for Galileo, Pythagoras' doctrines had a powerful effect upon him. He was a firm supporter of Copernicus and his scientific doctrine that displaced the Earth from the center of the cosmos and replaced it with the Sun—the heliocentric theory. But that theory was anathema to the Church with its doctrines of eternal unchangeability in the heavens and on Earth. The Inquisition is proof of that. Ecclesiastical Censure was placed upon Galileo:

> And whereas it has also come to the knowledge of the said Congregation that the Pythagorean doctrine—which is false and altogether opposed to the Holy Scripture—of the motion of the Earth, and the immobility of the Sun, which is also taught by Nicolaus Copernicus.... Because of such views His Holiness has directed the Lord Cardinal Bellarmine to summon before him the said Galileo and admonish him to abandon the said opinion; and, in case of his refusal to obey, that the Commissary is to enjoin him, before a notary and witnesses, a command to abstain altogether from teaching or defending this opinion and doctrine and even from discussing it; and, if he do not acquiesce therein, that he is to be imprisoned" (de Santillana, *Crime of Galileo,* 122–123).

However, for the scientists:

> A wide and wild leap it was, no doubt in those years around 1590: a perilous leap of the imagination into uncharted regions. No one but Galileo, and at the other end of Europe, Kepler, could see how it could make sense ultimately. But, as soon as their minds had grasped the idea, it became clear that this was a rebirth of the Pythagorean intuition of the unity of Nature.... It is what Galileo does not shy from calling by its proper name, the "Pythagorean philosophy".... But it was not before his sixtieth year that he dared to write that "the book of Nature

is written in mathematical characters." Thirty-five years of search...showed, not only on Earth, but throughout the universe, the "Pythagorean supposition" to be no supposition at all but corresponding to a state of fact. (ibid., 64–71)

Finally, Santillana notes:

> The slow growth of public interest in astronomy,...following the era of geographic discoveries...[allowed] the new idea...of the importance of natural science...to burst into flower. The heliocentric theory, under its ancient name of *Pythagorean philosophy*, had become common cultural property and common interest.... The last decree of the Inquisition had put a stop to all that...but common sense told Galileo that such a prohibition could not long survive. (ibid., 149–150)

One must honor Mr. De Santillana for writing such a book about Galileo. Many other books, written in the twentieth century, either omit the name of Pythagoras altogether, or paint Pythagoreanism with the broad brush of fantasy—a modern censure that can be traced back to the fanciful, even distorted philosophy of Philolaus. Aristotle had agreed the Pythagoreans sought mathematical proofs for their hypotheses, a fact that seems to have eluded most modern scholars. However, it took a great scientist, mathematician, and astronomer, Sir Thomas Heath, whose books were printed in 1913 and 1921 respectively, to set the record straight.

What comes to light is the fact that a very clear trajectory led back from Copernicus and Galileo (Kepler and Newton) to Pythagoras' heliocentric theory. Note: it does not seem to have crossed their minds that Philolaus was the inventor of such a theory. They understood that only a great scientist, mathematician and astronomer, with a flash of genius, could have discovered the heliocentric theory two thousand years before their own time! It took four of the greatest astronomer physicists of all time to vindicate Pythagoras. And, perhaps Pythagoras concealed his great discovery from the public from the understanding that he, too, like Socrates, and Galileo, after him, would be accused of believing in "gods" not accepted by the state.

KEPLER

As with Galileo, Kepler was forever avoiding religious persecution for his views. Let us be clear: changing the heavens, or even raising the issue was—dangerous! Pythagoras no doubt felt it in the sixth century BC. Socrates was accused of believing in "different gods" from those of the state, and this charge, though trumped up, was a major factor in his execution. Copernicus, like Darwin after him, waited more than twenty years before publishing his groundbreaking book, *De revolutionibus orbium coestium,* because he feared reprisals. Galileo was hauled before the Inquisition and made to [temporarily] recant his "heretical" view that the Sun is at the center of our solar system.

Johannes Kepler was a brilliant German mathematician and astronomer. Perhaps he, of all the great geniuses of the sixteenth and seventeenth centuries, had the direct insight to delve deeply into the doctrines of Pythagoras and the "Pythagoreans." Max Caspar, in his book, *Kepler,* states: "He wanted to write four cosmographical books. One about the universe, about the stationary parts of the universe, about the locus of the Sun and the fact that it is stationary, about the arrangement of the fixed stars and the fact that they are stationary, about the unity of the world and so forth." This book, *Mysterium Cosmographicum,* was described by Joscelyn Godwin in his invaluable book, *The Harmony of the Spheres,* as "the musical explanation of the cosmos" (Godwin, 221).

One could make the case that Kepler's researches were steeped from the very beginning in Pythagoras' discovery of the relation between musical intervals and planets of the solar system. For example, in chapter 12 of Kepler's *Mysterium Cosmographicum,* he broached the subject of the relation between the musical intervals, the Zodiac with its twelve parts, or houses, and the geometrical shapes of the Platonic solids. During Kepler's lifetime, only six planets had been identified, each with an orbit described as inhabiting its own concentric circle, and Kepler believed that, owing to the different radii of each planet from the Sun, it was possible to intersperse the five Platonic solids between the six planets and their spheres to create a whole and complete solar system. Kepler made his first experiments using circular planetary orbits in the classical Aristotelian mode, but when the ratios proved incorrect, he had the inspiration that the Earth is three-dimensional and that he should therefore adapt his research to planetary *spheres*. It was disappointing that the distances and ratios still did not prove correct between the planets and the Platonic solids, and Kepler was forced to abandon his hypothesis.

Fate played a part in the next phase of Kepler's life, because, although his endeavor with Platonic solids had failed, his reputation as a mathematician was secured by his book *Mysterium Cosmographicum*. In 1600, he was therefore invited to become assistant to the great observational astronomer, Tycho Brahe, in Prague, where he was given the task of understanding Mars' orbit, a particularly troublesome problem for astronomy at the time. Unfortunately Brahe exacerbated the problem by restricting Kepler's access to only a part of his voluminous observational data.

Fate stepped in again, because Brahe died a year later with the result that Kepler finally had access to the data that Brahe had withheld from him, and he set himself the task of determining once and for all the true orbit of Mars. Even with Brahe's remarkably precise observational material, it took six years of exacting research, beset by many wrong turns and dead ends, in order for Kepler to understand the elusive orbit of Mars. Along the way he tossed out the theory of equants, as well as that of epicycles in relation to planetary theory. In fact, as he closed in on the goal, his research led him even to depose the ancient Aristotelian doctrine that the orbits of the planets were *circular* in motion. What Kepler discovered, in a mood of jubilation, was that the planets had elliptical orbits!

Thus, Kepler's three laws of planetary motion were born: 1) The orbit of every planet is an ellipse with the Sun at a focus; 2) a line joining a planet and the Sun sweeps out equal areas during equal intervals of time; and 3) the square of the periodic times are to each other as the cubes of mean distances. Caspar adds:

> With his ellipse proposition, which defines the shape of the orbit of a planet, and the area proposition, which defines its form of motion, this law created an entirely new foundation for astronomical calculation. It is a great stride beyond Copernicus, who had been first to show how to obtain the *relative* distances

of the planets from the observations. For, while with him the ascertained values stand unrelated side by side, they now appear connected with each other by the periodic times, so that the entire number of the planets in truth presents itself *as a system* arranged by law. For Newton the law led to the statement of the law of gravitation. (Caspar, 286)

ISAAC NEWTON

The great seventeenth-century genius Sir Isaac Newton directly honored Pythagoras for having discovered the inverse-square law of planetary attraction that was so crucial to his own work on gravitation. As Joscelyn Godwin tells us in *The Harmony of the Spheres:*

> [Newton] saw himself less as an innovator than the rediscoverer of lost knowledge, the wisdom of antiquity and the *prisci theologi.* In the full daylight of the Scientific Revolution, there hovered in the background the familiar shades of Orpheus, Pythagoras, and Macrobius, as Newton seeks to demonstrate that the *Ancients already knew the inverse-square law of planetary attraction.* (Godwin, 305)

Godwin continues:

> In the 1690s Newton drafted a number of notes and learned comments (the "scholia") for a proposed second edition of his *Principia Mathematica;* our excerpt is from the classical Scholia to Propositions IV–IX of Book II. In the words of McGuire and Rattansi who first drew attention to these ideas: "Newton here asserts unequivocally that Pythagoras discovered by experiment an inverse–square relation in the vibrations of strings (unison of two strings when tensions are reciprocally as squares of lengths); that he extended such a relation to the weights and distances of the planets from the *Sun;* and that this true knowledge expressed esoterically, was lost through the misunderstanding of later generations." (ibid., 115)

From the *scholia,* Maguire and Rattansi transcribed "Newton and the 'Pipes of Pan'" in *Notes and Records of the Royal Society* (21 [1966],

108–143), in which they refer to the ancient authors Pliny, Pythagoras, Proclus, who had written about the musical intervals and how the esoteric knowledge related to the planets in our solar system. It begins thus:

> By what proportion gravity decreases by receding from the Planets the ancients have not sufficiently explained. Yet they appear to have adumbrated it by the harmony of the celestial spheres, designating the Sun and the remaining six planets, Mercury, Venus, Earth, Mars, Jupiter, Saturn, by means of Apollo with the Lyre of seven strings, and measuring the intervals of the spheres by the intervals of the tones.... Apollo's Lyre of seven strings provides understanding of the motions of all the celestial spheres over which nature has set the Sun as moderator...the Sun is called by the oracle of Apollo the King of the seven sounding harmony. But by this symbol they indicated that the Sun by his own force acts upon the planets in that harmonic ratio of distances by which the force of tension acts upon the strings of different lengths, that is reciprocally in the duplicate ratio of the distances. For the force by which the same tension acts on the same string of different lengths is *reciprocally as the square of the length of the string....*
>
> Now this argument is subtle, yet became known to the ancients. For Pythagoras, as Macrobius avows, stretched the intestines of sheep or the sinews of oxen by attaching the various weights, and from this learned the ratio of the celestial harmony. Therefore by means of such experiments he ascertained that the weights by which all tones on equal strings,...were reciprocally as the squares of the lengths of the string by which the musical instrument emits the same tones. *But the proportion discovered by these experiments*, on the evidence of Macrobius, he *applied to the heavens* and consequently by comparing those weights with the *weights* of the Planets and the lengths of the strings with the *distances* of the Planets, he understood by means of the harmony of the heavens that the weights of the Planets toward the *Sun were reciprocally as the squares of their distances from the Sun.*
>
> But the Philosophers loved so to mitigate their mystical discourses that in the presence of the vulgar they foolishly propounded vulgar matters from the sake of ridicule, and *hid the*

truth beneath discourses of this kind. In this sense *Pythagoras numbered his musical tones from the Earth,* as though from here to the Moon were a tone, and thence to a semitone, and from thence to the rest of the planets other musical intervals. *But he taught* that the sounds were emitted by the motion and attrition of the solid spheres, as though a greater sphere emitted a heavier tone as happens when iron hammers are smitten. And from this, it seems, was born the Ptolemaic system of solid orbs, when meanwhile *Pythagoras beneath parables of this sort was hiding his own system (i.e. heliocentric theory) and the true harmony of the heavens.* (ibid., 305–307)

One could not wish for a more authoritative confirmation of Pythagoras' remarkable discovery of the heliocentric planetary system than one of the other greatest scientific minds of all time, Sir Isaac Newton. It is touching that Newton saw himself "less as an innovator than as the re-discoverer of lost knowledge"—namely that the inverse-square law of planetary attraction operated in relation to the Sun, and that Pythagoras, had discovered the heliocentric theory two thousand years before it would be revived or, rediscovered by Nicholas Copernicus in the sixteenth century! We underscore that Newton mentioned only the name of Pythagoras as discovering the heliocentric theory of our solar system. We can therefore be certain, therefore, that one scientific genius, Newton, recognized in the mirror of antiquity another scientific genius by the name of Pythagoras!

We underscore, too, that there is no mention of Philolaus—not in the extracts from Macrobius, or Pliny, or Newton. And, when we bear in mind that he was not a mathematician, and merely had an interest in mathematics as it applied to the external world, it is quite clear that he had neither the intellect, the scientific, mathematical, or cosmological skills to have devised the true heliocentric theory. As stated, Philolaus displaced the Earth from the center of the cosmos for the central fire—a fanciful Presocratic notion disallowing any possibility of proof, since the central fire was invisible. His notion of the counter-earth was similarly invisible, and in hindsight, just as fanciful as his undefined, material, originating "principles" of limited and unlimited.

ust also point out that Philolaus was not speaking for the
rean school when he developed his theory. In fact, he was
a₁ ing to his Presocratic roots, but in a way that changed the Presocratic emphasis on the elements—water, air, fire, earth—for another
theory that argued for a "central fire" and an unlimited "continuum"
that perhaps echoes the Ionian, Anaximander. This in no way approxi-
mates the Pythagorean tenets in the document put forth by Alexander
Polyhistor, where the elements are ninth down the list from the Monad
(Monad, indefinite dyad, numbers, points, lines, planes, solid figures,
sensible bodies, and the elements.)

It is a sad comment that Aristotle believed the Pythagoreans held
vague, unprovable theories, whereas it was his inability to understand
or accept the metaphysical foundation of our cosmos that impeded him.
Unfortunately, the real center of that particular controversy was Philolaus, who apparently had access to some of the most secret Pythagorean theories, but altered them for his own Presocratic purposes while
still being honored under the Pythagorean banner.

CHAPTER 9

HARMONY OF THE SPHERES

The most misunderstood of Pythagoras' doctrines is the harmony of the spheres. And yet some of the greatest scientists, mathematicians and astronomers in history, have made major contributions to understanding this remarkable theory. Their names appear chronologically, and may convince us that the harmony of the spheres should not be dismissed as a fanciful dream.

Plato is, of course, the most conspicuous of Pythagoras' dedicated followers. Édouard Schuré tells us "he went to southern Italy to talk with the Pythagoreans, knowing full well that Pythagoras had been the greatest of Greek sages" (Schuré, 388). Plato did not focus intently on the harmony of the spheres, but one of the most discussed topics in philosophy is the creation of the World Soul found in Plato's *Timaeus* dialogue. Many scholars agree that although it has a very dense and cryptic form, the creation is patterned on Pythagorean ratios and proportions. In the case of the elements of our world, the dialogue tells us they, too, have a geometrical basis, in which *ideal, geometric* forms are the archetypes of the five Platonic solids.

They were all formed of convex regular polygons, with a different number of faces, according to the nature of each element as follows: The tetrahedron represents the element of fire; the cube, that of earth; the octahedron represents air; the icosahedron the element water, and the dodecahedron represents ether, the stuff of which the constellations and the heavens are made. There are exactly five solids. "These five shapes were looked upon with a sense of awe in ancient times...and they represented a pinnacle of ancient geometric and esoteric knowledge. Their construction comprised the final books of Euclid's *Elements*" (Hemenway, 150; see diagram next page).

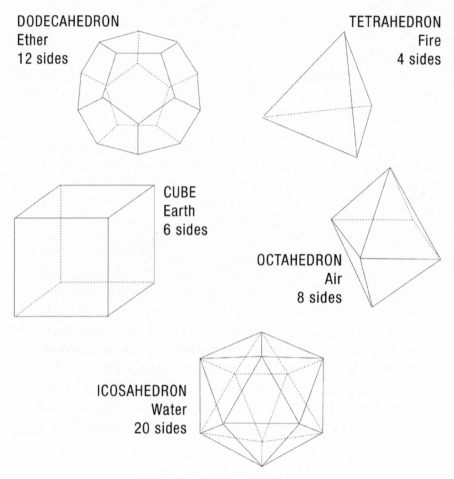

Five Platonic solids

Because the five Platonic solids were considered to be the core patterns, or archetypes of physical creation, and because God created them with mathematical precision and proportion in mind, these forms were considered to be "sacred geometry," a term used by archaeologists, anthropologists, and geometricians to encompass the religious, philosophical, and spiritual beliefs that have sprung up around geometry in various cultures during the course of human history.

Starting in the ancient world, and moving chronologically, we include the most important names of those who have focused on the question of the harmony of the spheres.

PLINY THE ELDER

Pliny the Elder (c. AD 24–79) is well known, even today, for writing a work *Natural History* in thirty-seven books, which would supply scientists and philosophers with material until well into the seventeenth century. He tells us:

> Many people have also attempted to discover the distances of the stars from the Earth, and have proclaimed that the Sun is nineteen times as far from the Moon as the Moon is to the Earth. *Pythagoras however*, a man of knowing soul, made the distance from the Earth to the Moon 126,000 stades, from the Moon to the Sun twice as much, and from the Sun to the twelve signs (of the Zodiac) three times. Our countryman Gallus Sulpicius was also of the same opinion. But sometimes *Pythagoras, using a musical theory*, calls the distance from the Earth to the Moon a whole tone, from the Moon to Mercury half as much, the same from Mercury to Venus, a tone and a half from Venus to the Sun, a tone from the Sun to Mars (i.e. the same as from the Earth to the Moon), half a tone from Mars to Jupiter, half a tone from Jupiter to Saturn, and a tone and a half from Saturn to the Zodiac. Thus it makes seven whole tones, which they call the harmony *diapason*, a universal harmony. (Godwin, 8)

NICOMACHUS OF GERASA

Nicomachus (c. AD 50–150) was another ancient thinker and mathematician whose *Introduction to Arithmetic* would later serve as a standard textbook for the medieval Christian and Islamic worlds. *The Enchiridion Harmonices "Textbook of Harmony"* includes the following:

> The breadth of Nicomachus' harmonic thought, embraced everything in the universal matrix of the musical Tetraktys (6:8:9:12, or the interval sequence E B A E) and the diatonic scale that fills it out: the movements of the planets, the acoustics of instruments, Pythagoras' discoveries, experiments, and innovation, and Plato's creation of the World Soul. The harmony of tone with number became, for the Pythagoreans, a kind of

Grand Unified Theory; an archetype of the harmony which permeates and unites both the greater and the lesser world.

His story of Pythagoras is the stuff not of mere history but of genuine myth. *It records the semi-divine origin of harmonic knowledge,* replete with hints of deeper meaning. (Godwin, 9)

However, his greatest contribution is his account of what precise scientific steps Pythagoras took to discover the musical intervals of octave, fifth, and fourth that became the foundation and basis of the harmony of the spheres, the heliocentric theory, and of all Western music.

Before relating the report of Pythagoras' discovery, it is important to contextualize it within the relationship of the seven-stringed lyre and the eight-stringed lyre, which Pythagoras is said by Nicomachus to have invented. The explanation for that invention is stated in the section on Nichmachus as follows:

Pythagoras was the first who sought to avoid the middle note of the conjunct tetrachords (being the same distance—a fourth—from the two extremes *hypate* and *nete*), in order *to obtain a more varied system*, as we may suppose, and also to *make the extremes themselves produce the most satisfying consonances*, the octave-ratio of 2:1. *This could not be the case with the existing tetrachords.* He therefore intercalated an eighth note between the *mese* and *paramese* and fixed it at the distance of a whole tone from the *mese*, a semitone from the *paramese*. In this way, the string which previously represented the *paramese* in the heptachordal lyre was still called *trite*—'third' counting from the *nete*—and still occupies this position, while the intercalated string was fourth from the *nete* and sounds a fourth with it: a consonance which was originally sounded between the mese and hypate...25. The note (B) placed between these two—the *mese* and the intercalated string—received the name of the former *paramese*...it furnished the consonance of a fifth, marking the limits of a system formed by the tetrachord itself plus the added tone. Thus the sesquitertia ratio (3:2) of the fifth is acknowledged as the sum of the sesquitertia and the sesquioctave or whole tone (4:3 times 9:8).

Chapter 6. 26. As for the numerical quantity which represents the distance of the strings sounding the fourth, fifth, and their sum, the octave—in fact the additional note placed between the two tetrachords—here is how Pythagoras is said to have reported its discovery. (Godwin, 12)

He [Pythagoras] happened by a providential coincidence to pass by a blacksmith's workshop, and heard quite clearly the iron hammers striking on the anvil.... He recognized among these sounds the consonances of the diapason [octave], diapente (fifth), and the (fourth)....

28. Thrilled, he entered the shop as if a god were aiding his plans, and after various experiments discovered that it was the difference of weights that caused the differences of pitch, and not the effort of the worked iron. With greatest of care he ascertained the weights of the hammers and their impulsive force, which he found perfectly identical, then returned home.

29. He fixed a single nail in the angle formed by two walls in order to avoid even here the slightest difference, and lest the number of nails having each their own substance might invalidate the experiment. From this nail he hung four strings identical in substance, number of threads, thickness, and torsion, and suspended from the lower end of each of them a weight. He made the lengths of the strings, moreover, exactly the same, then, plucking them together two by two, he heard the previously mentioned consonances that varied with each pair of strings.

30. The string stretched by the greatest weight compared to that which supported the smallest, sounded the interval of an octave. Now the former represented twelve units of the given weight, and the latter, six. *He thus proved that the octave is in duple ratio,* as the weights themselves had made him suspect. The greatest string compared to the next smallest, representing eight units, sounded the fifth and he proved that they were in sesquitertia ratio, that being the ratio of the weights. Then he compared it to the next one, with regard to the weight it supported. The larger of the two other strings, having nine units, sounded the fourth, so he established that it was in the inverse sesquitertia ratio, and that this same string was in sesquialtera ratio to the smallest—for 9 to 6 is the same ratio, just as the second smallest string with 8 units is in sesquitertia ratio to the one of six units, and in sesquialtera ratio to the one of twelve units.

31. Consequently, the interval between the fifth and the fourth—the amount by which the fifth exceeds the fourth—was confirmed as being in the sesquioctave ratio (9:8). The octave system was formed by the union of one and the other, namely the fifth and the fourth placed side by side. So the double ratio is composed of the sesquialters and sesquiterta 12:8:6 or inversely, by the union of the fourth and fifth, so that the octave is composed of the sesquitertia and sesquialtera in this order, 12:9:6.

32. After having exercised his hand and his ear in the study of the suspended weights, and having established from these weights the *ratios of the proportion stated*, he ingeniously transferred the results obtained through strings hung on a nail placed in the angle of a wall to the soundboard of an instrument he called "cordotone" in which the tension, raised to a point proportional to that which the weights produced, passed to the movement of pegs placed in the upper part. Once installed on this terrain, and possessing, as it were, an infallible gnomon, he enlarged the experiment by making it on different instruments: for example, by striking vases, on flutes, syrinxes, monochords, trigons and suchlike. *He invariably found the numerical determination consonant and reliable.*

33. He called the note corresponding to the number 6 *hypate*; the note of 8, a sesquiteria above, *mese*; the note of 9, a tone higher than the mean and consequently is sesquioctave, *paramese*; and finally 12 he called *nete*. Then he supplied the intermediary points according to the diatonic genus by means of proportional notes and thus bound the *octachord* lyre to the consonant numbers, namely the double, the sesquialtera, the sesquitertia, and the difference between the latter pair, the sesquioctave.

35. Thus in the heptachordal lyre, *previous to this one*, every fourth note starting from the lowest one was always a fourth away, the semitone occupying by turns, according to its placement, the first degree, the middle degree, and the third degree of the tetrachord. But in the *Pythagorean, or octachordal lyre*, there is either—in the case of conjunction—a system composed of a tetrachord and a pentachord, or—in the case of disjunction—two tetrachords separated by the interval of a tone. Thus the progression from the lowest string will be such that *every*

fifth note is consonant by the interval of a fifth, the semitone occupying by turns four different degrees: the first, second, third, and fourth. (ibid., 9–14)

THEON OF SMYRNA

[Theon of Smyrna (ca. AD 115–140)] viewed mathematics not as a self-sufficient science but as an entry to the world of real, divine, and almost personified numbers which in the Pythagorean and Platonic worldview embody the ultimate laws of the universe....

After having finished our treatise on mathematics, we will add to it a dissertation on the harmony of the world and will not hesitate to relate what our predecessors have discovered, nor to make more widely known the Pythagorean traditions which we have inherited, without ourselves claiming to have discovered the least part of it....

According to the doctrine of Pythagoras, the world being indeed harmoniously ordained, the celestial bodies which are distant from one another according to the proportions of consonant sounds, create, by the movement and speed of their revolutions the corresponding harmonic sounds. (ibid., 16–18)

PTOLEMY

One might be surprised to see the name of the great Ptolemy (AD 127–148) included in this discussion of the harmony of the spheres, since we usually associate him solely with his great astronomical achievements.

His works on astronomy (the *Almagest*), astrology (the *Tetrabiblos*) and geography became standard texts for the Arabic, Byzantine, and Western Middle Ages. After Aristotle, he was the major scientific authority for the Medieval period....

The first and second books of Ptolemy's *Harmonics* are an ordinary treatise on scales and intervals. With the third chapter of Book III the tone suddenly changes to that of a fantasia on psychic and cosmic harmony...Ptolemy is quite eloquent about the wonder and awe which the study of harmonics arises....

[i.e.] unlocking the doors of insight into a numbered and harmonious universe, in which microcosm and macrocosm reflect in time and space endless variations on a central theme. At the end of Book III, Chapter 5, he correlates the seven faculties of the soul and the seven virtues of reason with the seven notes of the scale. (ibid., 21–22)

In chapter 4 Ptolemy states that harmonic power appears most clearly in the human soul and the movements of the stars, and in chapter 5 he seeks to know how the consonant intervals correspond to the original diversity of the soul's powers. In chapter 8, he summarizes:

We found that the identical and consonant intervals were constructed in correspondence with the original parts of the soul, the divisions of the *emmeleis* agreed with the division of the virtues, the generic differences of the tetrachords with those of the virtues according to value and size, and the modulations with the changing moods in the course of life. It remains to compare with these the movements of the stars, which are accomplished according to harmonic laws....

What was established...is that the same relationships hold for the position of the diameter of the circle as for what was said of the octave. For the ratio 2:1 denotes in this comparison the ratio of the circle to the semi-circle...the diameter divides both the area and the circumference into two equal parts. (ibid., 29–31)

Ptolemy then plots the Greek musical scale onto a Linear Zodiac, discusses the consonant intervals in relation to aspects in the zodiac, how the movement of the stars accords with rising and falling, and modulation, and how the "arrangement of the tetrachords in the Perfect System agrees with the arrangement of the aspects with regard to the Sun" (ibid., 29–37). In addition Ptolemy states:

We can compare the fixed tones to the position of just these numbers, as follows: *proslambanomenos* with the 180-degree position, *hypate meson* with 120 degrees, *nete diezeumenon* with 90 degrees, and *nete hyperbolain* with 60 degrees" (ch. 15). Under these conditions the number of the square (in astrology/astronomy) is 90; the mean between 120; the number of the trine; and 60, the number of the sextile; and it produces two ratios, 3:2 and 4:3, in accordance with the first consonant intervals, the fifth and the fourth. As in music these first consonant intervals, the fifth and the fourth, together make the octave identity, so also the two ratios mentioned, 3:2 and 4:3, produce the ratio 2:1 in conformity with the octave identity.... If we now recall the polygons, namely the triangle, square, and hexagon, the corresponding ratios in harmony can also be deduced, partly from the number of their angles, partly from other features which may present themselves. (ibid., 37–39)

There are many more remarkably precise correlations between the musical intervals and the planetary movements, such as to wonder whether Ptolemy had not the best grasp of Pythagoras' doctrines until the time of Kepler, and even then to wonder whether he had not presented that material in a truly transparent light.

MACROBIUS

Macrobius (ca. AD 400) had many interests including astronomy, music theory and the Neo-Platonic doctrine of the soul—doctrines which echoed down into the Middle Ages. As Godwin notes, "the treatment of music, given here in its entirety, encompasses skillfully all the main points of the Pythagorean-Platonic musical worldview" (ibid., 64). Macrobius begins by discussing the World-Soul as found in Plato's *Timaeus,* and then moves along into a discussion "in the *Republic* about the whirling motion of the heavenly spheres. Plato says that a Siren sits upon each of the spheres thus indicating that by the motions of the spheres divinities were provided with a song; for a singing Siren is equivalent to a god in the Greek acceptance of the word. Moreover, cosmologists have chosen to consider the Nine Muses as the tuneful song of the eight spheres and the one predominant harmony that comes from all of them" (ibid., 65–66).

Macrobius also refers to Porphyry, a Neo-Platonist of the third century AD, as saying that Platonists "believed that the intervals in the corporeal universe, which were filled with sesquitertians, sesquialters, superoctaves, halftones, and a *leimma,* followed the pattern of the Soul's fabric...the proportional intervals of which were interwoven into the fabric of the Soul and were also injected into the corporeal universe which is quickened by the Soul" (ibid., 68).

PROCLUS

Proclus [AD 410–485] was head of the Athenian Academy and one of the last and greatest lights of classical Neo-Platonism. He believed himself to be a reincarnation of Nicomachus of Gerasa and, as a deeply philosophical syncretist, expanded Platonism into a vast system capable of accomodating all religions without contradiction. The Athenian Academy ended its ninth-century career shortly after his death. (ibid., 71)

In this extract from Proclus' commentary on the *Republic*, he clarifies the status of the Sirens, who in Plato's myth stand upon the spheres uttering each a tone. Proclus distinguishes the Sirens from the Muses.

Each one [Siren] gives forth a single sound whose one tone, being in perfect agreement with the musical ratios signifies the unity of the sound and the total simplicity of the noise which they make...since the rings and the Sirens are eight in number, he says that there results from this ensemble a single harmony...it is as if the Sirens' workings resembled the sound from which results the interval of an octave, which is the most complete of all...Plato has named these souls "Sirens" in order to show that the chord which they impose on the rings is, nevertheless, of a corporeal nature. He has called them "celestial Sirens."... The commentary on the *Timaeus*, as it survives, covers only the first part of Plato's text (up to 44-b) dealing with the creation of the World Soul.... He has situated the creative process...within a broader and truly universal context. He therefore reminds us that creative actions that might seem to be primordial and autonomous are in turn indebted to yet higher models, to which the Demiurge looked in dividing the soul. (ibid., 73–71)

Thus, "another of Proclus' concerns is to maintain the idea of the soul's unity, despite its division: 'The essence therefore of the soul is at one and the same time a whole, and has parts, and is one and multitude.' . . . Running through the whole work is Proclus' ambition to make a *Harmony of Orpheus, Pythagoras, and Plato* by commenting on Plato's writings in the light of Orphic and Chaldean theology and Pythagorean arithmology" (ibid., 75–72).

Despite the end of the Athenian Academy with the death of Proclus, the interest in Pythagoras' harmony of the spheres continued to interest serious scholars through the centuries. In the Medieval period we find John Scotus Erigena (c.815—877), and Al-Hasan al-Katib (fl. c.1000) "who was part of the Pythagorean-Platonic tradition as it was being continued in the world of Islam" (ibid., 120).

"In music, this meant especially the Pythagorean insight into number, and the proportions between numbers, as being the key to the universe" (ibid., 120). In the Renaissance period it includes Marsilio Ficino, who was fated to meet Cosimo de Medici in Florence around the year 1439. Cosimo had been inspired to collect all possible manuscripts of ancient Greek philosophy, and he commissioned Marcilio Ficino to translate them from Greek into Latin. Ficino began by translating the *Corpus Hermeticum* attributed to Hermes Trismegistus, and then he proceeded to translate all the works of Plato. As Godwin notes, "Ficino was appointed at a young age as head of a revived Platonic Academy" (ibid., 163). In the Baroque period it included Robert Fludd, Marin Mersenne, Angelo Berardi, and its most celebrated star Johannes Kepler.

Notice that on the particular topic of the harmony of the spheres, the great astronomers Copernicus and Galileo are absent.

JOHANNES KEPLER

Kepler (1571–1630) was perhaps unique among the great geniuses of the sixteenth and seventeenth centuries in that in his pursuit of the harmony of the spheres and the planetary orbits he was deeply inspired by Pythagoras' doctrines from the start.

In Kepler's earlier work, *Mysterium Cosmographicum* he had broached the subject of the connection between the musical intervals, the geometrical shapes of the Platonic solids and the sectioning of the Zodiac into twelve parts, or "houses." But, despite the fact that Kepler had first used the Aristotelian circular planetary orbits and later adapted his research to planetary spheres, the ratios and distances between the planets and Platonic solids still proved to be too imprecise and he abandoned that theory. However, when Kepler finally had access to the volumes of very precise observational data that Brahe had withheld from him, and after many years of exacting work, he discovered that Mars (and the other planets) had elliptical orbits.

Kepler was now deeply inspired to understand the Harmony of the World, and his researches went far beyond astronomy. His great work, *Harmonice Mundi* was a remarkable endeavor to show that God's presence in the heavens and the Earth was reflected in the mathematical congruence of diverse categories found in nature, music, and the solar system.

Polyhedra

In chapters 1 and 2 of *Harmonice Mundi*, Kepler greatly extended his examination of the polyhedra (the geometric figures) comprising the Platonic solids, with the specific intention to rank them according to their congruence. He describes the polyhedra in terms of their faces, adopting Plato's description in the *Timaeus*, and his mathematical description of the small stellated dodecahedron and the great stellated dodecahedron earned the name Kepler's solids. In the case of magnitudes, Kepler was guided by the ancient Greek discovery in the sixth century BC of the existence of irrational numbers, which although finite in extension, are nonetheless incommensurable—i.e., do not share any common measure with whole or natural numbers. Kepler devised a system for classifying both the commensurable and incommensurable magnitudes into a system of "degrees of knowability" using the circle as a relative unit of measure.*

Nature

Kepler sought the geometrical congruences in everyday objects whose mathematical relations had been unknown or overlooked. "In a paragraph toward the end of his 1611 essay *On the Six Cornered Snowflake* Kepler mentions the 'Divine Proportion' [Golden section] and the 'Fibonacci sequence' in practically the same breath as flowers and pentagons. It is in the likeness of this self-developing series

---

* Information from http://www.keplersdiscovery.com (accessed 9/12/17).

that the faculty of propagation is, in my opinion, manifest: and so in a flower the authentic flag of this faculty is shown, the pentagon" (ibid.).

In the Fibonacci sequence, each number is the sum of the two preceding numbers, and Kepler found this series was the foundational structure of pinecones, the hearts of Sunflowers, and many other species of plants. As Priya Hemenway notes: "If we look at the numbers in the Fibonacci sequence and find the ratios between successive numbers, we will see that they approach the Divine Proportion—namely 1.618033988749848 etc." As for Divine Proportion itself: "The whole is to the larger in exactly the same proportion as the larger is to the smaller." In the case of roses, "an angle that is congruent to 360 degrees by the Divine Proportion (137.5°) separates the petals from one another" (Hemenway, 135).

As the title suggests, knowledge of divine proportion can transform one's understanding of the world around us—it is revealed in the Parthenon, the Great Pyramid of Giza, the Rose Window of Chartres Cathedral, in the Vitruvian Man of Leonardo da Vinci, the Statue of David by Michaelangelo, the polyhedra of the dodecahedron, the shape of a snowflake, a pinecone, a rose, and even that of the universe itself.

Music

Kepler's *Harmony of the World* was in essence an attempt to show that diverse classifications of actual things found on Earth, (in Nature), and the heavens (our planetary system) were in *congruence with the foundational ratios of music,* discovered by Pythagoras in the sixth century BC—namely the octave (2:1), the fifth (3:2), and the fourth (4:3).

Kepler's exacting researches led him to add other ratios/proportions as follows: major sixth (4:5); minor sixth (5:8); major third (4:5) and minor third (5:6). What Kepler discovered was that "just as planetary orbits were not based on perfect circles, the principles underlying harmony had infinitesimal discrepancies, such as 1/81 of an octave, called a "comma." Whereas Galileo sought to "split the difference"— i.e., to temper the notes to equal tuning, Kepler discovered that the principles of harmony could not be reduced in that way without sacrificing true consonance. Therefore, with the above additions, *the musical foundations discovered by Pythagoras remained as the basis for harmony sought by Kepler.*

Solar System

Kepler, and Pythagoras before him, sought harmonic proportions in the solar system. He had already, in the *Mysterium Cosmographicum* searched for the congruence between the Platonic solids and the Zodiac. After years of research Kepler had concluded the ratios and distances were imprecise, but he did not dispose of his trust in the harmony of the planetary system. In the *Harmonice Mundi* he merely looked for other avenues by which to prove it. He sought to find whether the greatest and least *distances* of a planet from the Sun might approximate harmonic ratios, but they did not. He then applied the same principle regarding fastest and slowest *speeds* of a planet from the Sun, and he discovered that the planets *did* seem to approximate harmonies with respect to their own orbits" (cf. footnote, page 118).

Seeking still more precise harmonies, he examined the ratios between the fastest or slowest speed of a planet and slowest and fastest speed of its neighbors (which he calls "converging" and "diverging" motions). He discerned harmonies in each case with discrepancies smaller than a *"diesis,"* of 24/25, the smallest harmonic interval that a human ear can discern.

Kepler discovered, he believed, that *harmonic relationships structure the characteristics of the planetary orbits individually and their relationship to one another.* The only interval that diverged slightly (by 18/19) was that between Mars and Jupiter, but the discovery of the asteroid belt between those two planets was seen as the likely reason for that discrepancy. As Godwin notes, "The recent researches of Rudolf Haase show that the predominance of harmonious intervals in the solar system, as discovered by Kepler, not only far exceeds random expectation, *but is reinforced by measurement of the outer planets that were not yet discovered in Kepler's day"* (Godwin, 222).

Let us state, therefore, that Kepler not only confirmed but also *demonstrated* Pythagoras' theory that harmonic relationships structure the planetary orbits individually and their relationship to one another. As

Pythagoras discovered in the sixth century BC, the cosmos is based on principles of music as reflected in mathematical ratios and proportion!

ALBERT FREIHERR VON THIMUS

I began this chapter by pointing out that the most misunderstood of Pythagoras' doctrines was the harmony of the spheres and that many important historical figures over the centuries had contributed to the research on this mysterious and arcane subject. Kepler's book *Harmony of the World* was an inspired attempt to show that the diverse classifications of actual things found on Earth (in Nature) and the heavens (our planetary system) *were in congruence with the foundational ratios of music* discovered by Pythagoras in the sixth century BC.

The work of Albert Freiherr von Thimus (1806–1878) reveals the ongoing nature of this mystery. As preparation he studied the I Ching, the Tao Te Ching, Egyptian hieroglyphs, Greek philosophy, the Church Fathers and Doctors, and music theory since the Middle Ages.

> Von Thimus had the insight that the one unifying symbolic factor behind all ancient lore and learning might have been the discovery of the harmonic series and its association with mathematics.... For him, it is an example of how the esoteric harmonic doctrine came first, then the cosmic picture—in this case, that of the heliocentric system known in Antiquity. (Godwin, 370–371)

The Pythagorean Table (see diagram next page) provides a visual representation of Von Thimus's theory that is too long and esoteric to be outlined fully in this short homage to his work. The full account can be found in Godwin's invaluable book, *The Harmony of the Spheres* (pp. 370–381).

He concludes, however, that "In order for the spiritual contemplation of harmonic numbers (*not the physical perception of tonal phenomena*) to bring to consciousness the formative norms of harmonic laws, the series of the *perissos*-ratios of the major chord and those of the *artios*-ratios of the minor chord, must ideally begin not with the measuring of one actual number as always large or small, but with the concept of the One in itself and with the forms of the

Unbounded Duality of infinite quantity itself" (Godwin, 372). Von Thimus thus mirrors the doctrine of Pythagoras found in the Alexander Polyhistor template:

> The principle of all things is the monad or unit;
> Arising from this monad the undefined dyad, or two,
>   serves as material substratum, which is cause;
> From the monad and the undefined dyad spring numbers.

Has Pythagoras proved himself *still* to be centuries ahead of the times? We shall see!

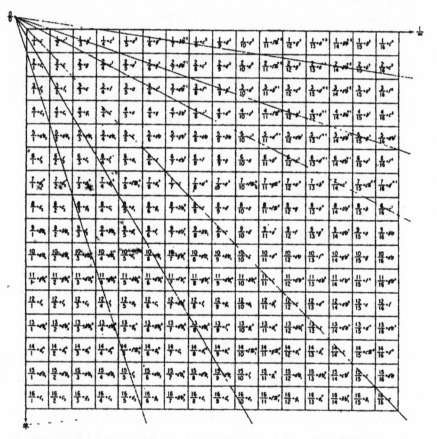

The Pythagorean Table (Godwin, The Harmony of the Spheres)

CHAPTER 10

ASTRONOMY

Huffman begins his chapter on Philolaus astronomical system by making an important announcement.

> The only fragments which are relevant to the astronomical system (of Philolaus) are fragments 7 and 17, which I have already discussed in relation to Philolaus' cosmology. They show that the cosmos is a sphere and that there is a fire at the center. On the other hand, the details of the astronomical system are all derived from secondary sources, of which there are two main types:
>
> First there is Aristotle (texts 1, 2, 5).... This tradition knows of only one Pythagorean astronomical system, the one that includes the central fire, and that system is always ascribed to Pythagoreans in general, with no mention of any individual Pythagoreans....
>
> The second source for early Pythagorean astronomy is the doxographical tradition represented by Aetius, which ultimately goes back to Aristotle's pupil, Theophrastus (texts 7–9). Here we find the same astronomical system mentioned in Aristotle, but this time it is ascribed to Philolaus. (Huffman, 242)

Immediately we are faced with challenges. The first is *that there are no relevant astronomical fragments ascribed to Philolaus himself.* This is a remarkable, even astounding statement.

The second challenge, from the very outset, is that Huffman tells us that there are two schools of thought pertaining to Pythagorean astronomy. The first is associated with Aristotle himself, and ascribes the Pythagorean system to the Pythagoreans in general—i.e., not naming Philolaus as the author. The second school of thought comes from the doxographical tradition, involving both Aetius and Theophrastus (successor to Aristotle at the Lyceum) who are themselves part of the Aristotelian tradition, yet are willing to break with his authority in ascribing the Pythagorean astronomical system to Philolaus.

When we consider the input from the Presocratics, these two different versions of the Pythagorean astronomical system; Aristotle's possible conflicts with Philolaus; the doxographical tradition in general, (to say nothing of a plentitude of commentators throughout the ages since ancient Greece), the way ahead appears to be through a dense thicket of diverse opinions. Nonetheless, the big question remains. Can *we* assume that the astronomical system proposed by Philolaus corresponds to that of Pythagoras?

Huffman begins the section entitled Astronomy by telling us that "it (Philolaus' planetary system) has been subject to the widest range of assessments imaginable, but the true nature of its contribution to the development of *Presocratic* thought has seldom been appreciated" (ibid., 240). He mentions the criticisms of well-known commentators such as Frank and van der Waerden as believing the system to be so sophisticated that it could not be the work of Philolaus in the latter part of the fifth century, but should be attributed to someone in the fourth century. Burkert and Dicks have shown, says Huffman, that the system was not as sophisticated as Frank and van der Waerden had contended and that it had, in fact, close ties to the thought of other fifth-century authors such as Empedocles and Anaxagoras. Huffman adds that Burkert also "went to the opposite extreme and argued, 'The Philolaic system is simply mythology in scientific clothing'" (ibid., 241). What are we to make of all this?

Huffman introduces his own view by stating quite clearly:

My own thesis is his [Burkert's] attempt to turn the Philolaic system into myth or fantasy is misguided. To be sure, the system is *not a mathematically sophisticated* account of planetary motion either, but it is clearly a product of the tradition of Presocratic thought on the cosmos. Despite its *peculiarities (central fire, counter-earth) it can account for all the phenomena that the systems of Anaxagoras, Empedocles and Democritus can,* and is in fact more sophisticated in that it recognizes just the five canonical planets rather than an indefinite number. It is in fact the most impressive example of Presocratic speculative astronomy and *establishes Philolaus as an important precursor of Plato.* (ibid., 241)

This is indeed a glowing testimonial of Philolaus' astronomical achievements. Our purpose, however, is not to locate Philolaus within the *Presocratic* tradition, but to see whether his system corresponds with that of *Pythagoras*, since he is historically credited with being a Pythagorean and a possible successor to Pythagoras.

Huffman continues by giving an overview of Philolaus' system. He has already informed us that the only fragments which are relevant to the astronomical system are fragments 7 and 17, which relate to Philolaus' cosmology (ibid., 242), a fact that might immediately create misgivings. Why? Because Huffman has mentioned a "reconstructed" cosmos full of astronomical facts never mentioned by Philolaus himself! One such fact refers to fragment 17 which states, among other things, that "the world order is one," a statement which clearly contradicts Philolaus' other claim, that the origins of the world are plural unlimiteds and limiters, which arose from and are an integral part of Nature.

As to the planetary system itself, Huffman announces:

> At first sight the system described in the testimonia is impressive for its symmetry and audacity: *"The Earth is removed* from its traditional place in the center of the cosmos and moves in a circular orbit like the other planets. However, the center of the cosmos is not the Sun but a mysterious central fire which is called the hearth."* (ibid., 243)

This notion of the central fire, upon which Huffman places the focus of his entire planetary system, needs to be reviewed.

The first thing one notes is that when Huffman introduces his own views, above, he realizes that the central fire and the counter-earth are *peculiarities,* meaning he knows they do not fit into any known scientific planetary theory. And yet, Huffman continues: "Despite its peculiarities it *can account for all the phenomena* that the systems of Anaxagoras, Empedocles and Democritus can," revealing that we are to view Philolaus' account within the Presocratic tradition. Huffman tells us the central fire is *invisible,* yet it holds the central place in the known universe, and all the planets, including Earth, move in a circular orbit around it. This is indeed a most cavalier statement!

Huffman then introduces some information we might at first have overlooked. He tells us that the *doxographical tradition* (referring to Testimonium A16) maintains that *there was fire at the periphery of the cosmos* as well as at the center" (ibid., 245). In fact, part of Testimonium A16 reads: "*Philolaus says* there is fire in the middle around the center which he calls the hearth of the whole and house of Zeus (see 16b). And *again another fire at the uppermost place surrounding the whole*" (ibid., 237). One does wonder what Aetius meant by "there is a fire in the middle *around* the center," as well as his latter statement. However, these alleged "facts" will never be corroborated by science.

Testimonium A17 notes, "The inhabited Earth is third (from the central fire) and lies opposite to and moves around with the counter-earth. Accordingly *those on the counter-earth cannot be seen by those on this Earth*" (ibid., 238). Here Philolaus is stating that there are inhabitants on the counter-earth, a statement, which, to a scientist, is pure fantasy.

This position ties in with the following statement, which follows on criticism of Philolaus' account of the cosmos. Similarly, the most recent work on Presocratic cosmology concludes that "the system of Philolaus makes very little astronomical sense, and it is hard to believe that it was intended to do so," and asserts that with Philolaus' account of the *inhabitants of the Moon* (A20), "the whole scheme lapses into fantasy" (Furley, 1987; ibid., 241). Testimoniam A20 *actually* states, "Some of the Pythagoreans, including Philolaus, say that the Moon appears earth-like *because it is inhabited,* with animals and plants which are greater and finer. For (he says) that the animals on it are fifteen-fold in power...and that the day is...fifteen times an earth day" (Huffman, 270). I would have expected A20 to be collected together with the other testimonia mentioned above, but it is thirty pages away in Huffman's book. Instead Huffman appeals to Testimonium A21 which states ("On the Motion of the Earth"): "Others say that the Earth is stationary. But Philolaus the Pythagorean that it moves in a circle around the fire according to an inclined circle in the same way as the Sun and Moon" (ibid., 238).

No doubt it was statements like these that caused Burkert to argue "that the Philolaic system is simply 'mythology in scientific clothing'" (1972: 342). Or, perhaps, fantasy in scientific clothing. In short, the statements made in the doxographical tradition are such as to seriously undermine Philolaus' view of himself as an astronomer, especially one that Huffman places as a precursor to Plato.

Huffman continues, giving the essential distillation of Philolaus' planetary system found in his long, dense, often obfuscating book (diagram, page 90). "Ten bodies circle around the central fire, starting from the outside there are first the fixed stars, followed by five planets [no specified order], the Sun, the Moon, the Earth and finally the counter-earth" (ibid., 244). Huffman also tells us:

> Philolaus can be seen as adopting the spherical shape for the cosmos which was *probably* first clearly set out by Parmenides. [As Heath shows, it was *Pythagoras* who first discovered the spherical shape of the cosmos, a word he also coined.]...
>
> The Earth is the second body out from the center after the counter-earth. However we never see either the central fire nor the counter-earth because the Earth rotates once on its axis as it orbits around the central fire, thus keeping one side of the Earth always turned away from the center. All of the bodies moving around the central fire have one circular motion from west to east. The Earth's motion is far faster than the Moon, Sun, and five planets, since it completes its circuit around the central fire in twenty-four hours. Its motion thus accounts for the apparent movement of the Sun across the sky (and hence for night and day) as well as the apparent nightly movement of the Moon, stars, and planets from east to west. The Earth's orbit is inclined to that of the Sun, Moon, and planets, and this inclination accounts for the apparent movement of the Sun higher and lower in the sky and hence accounts for the seasons. The movement of the counter-earth is not made clear, but *presumably* since its name suggests that it is paired with the Earth, it moves at a similar velocity and at the same angle to the plane of the motion of the Sun and other planets.
>
> The Sun, Moon, and planets then have one circular motion from west to east which is much slower (in angular velocity at

least) than that of the Earth and which explains their observed motion from west to east through the zodiac. The Moon completes its circuit in about a month, the Sun in a year and each of the planets progressively slower. The idea would then seem to be that the farther away from the center the body is the slower it moves. The system is thus very simple and elegant, postulating just one motion for each body with all the motions being in the same direction, although that of the Earth is in a plane inclined to that of the rest. Such a system will explain the astronomical phenomena that are *most commonly known*...but fails to account for retrograde motion, a phenomena not explained by any Presocratic theory. (ibid., 244–254)

COMMENTARY

Huffman states in fragment 7 that the "first thing fitted together, the one at the center of the sphere is called the hearth." (The central fire, the hearth, is now at the center of the cosmos, deposing the Earth from that position.) Let us unpack that statement. The hearth is a mysterious, invisible, "planetary body" akin to a Sun since it governs all the known planets in Philolaus' cosmos. It may be the first thing "fitted together" but it does not precede Philolaus' *originating* sets of unknown principles, the limiters and the unlimiteds. Let us bear in mind that Philolaus' unlimiteds and limiters are *material* principles, derived from and part of the structure of Nature. It is impossible that unknown *material* principles can "create" the central fire because it is an *invisible* principle, and it takes on the cloak of "quasi-transcendence" because it is now an *invisible principle* that governs Philolaus' cosmos for which he cannot scientifically account.

In addition, although the hearth is the first thing "fitted together," it is given the place of honor at the center of the cosmos, due to its placement at the "center of the sphere." But Philolaus makes no mention of the *origin* of the sphere; whether it "just happened to be there" when the hearth was fitted together, or whether it was fitted together afterward. The hearth cannot be purely unlimited because it takes limiters and unlimiteds to create the cosmos, and we have been told that it is the crucial—and undefined—*harmonia* which is responsible for harmonizing these opposing principles into the world order.

In Philolaus' hypothesis the sphere plays nothing but a tangential part, and I would point out that according to Heath it was *Pythagoras* who first defined the sphere; it was the shape of all celestial objects, including the Earth; and the definition was arrived at by way of science and mathematics, not fanciful, unprovable speculations.

If as Philolaus suggests, the central fire is defined as the center of the cosmos *because* of its position within the sphere, then he has encased an *unlimited,* the fire (but an "element"), within a sphere, which would be defined as a *limiter* because a sphere is a mathematical definition in terms of the Earth. Such a hypothesis is quite un-provable because the central fire is *invisible.* In addition, what are we to make of Philolaus' claim that the originating cosmic principles are limiters and unlimiteds? Are they now subsidiary to "the first thing fitted together, the central fire"? (fragment 7). The central fire, the hearth, rules the cosmos.

As we noted, for Aristotle *from the one and single unlimited,* the universe drew forth the limiters—time, breath, and void, to which Huffman added Philolaus' musical intervals and the harmonia (which were both discovered by *Pythagoras*!). On that view it is impossible for an unlimited, the invisible central fire, to be materially enclosed by anything, much less a limiter, in this case because of its relation to the sphere. Here it would appear that Philolaus has turned Aristotle's doctrine about Unlimited/Limit upside down. Again, it is implied in Philolaus' own "system" that the central fire is both unlimited and limited—a problem, especially if fire is an element and not an a priori originating principle. Last, and most crucial, the central fire cannot be known much less defined, even by Philolaus, because in his system it is an invisible element, as is confirmed by Huffman's comment that the whole of the celestial world including the fixed stars and planets, orbit this invisible central fire. But, the obvious should be stated: at that historical period an element, even fire, could not be invisible on Presocratic grounds of seeking the natural origins of our world. Nor could the hypothesis of the central fire ever be proved. In short, it is a quasi Presocratic speculation, but it rests upon the mathematical and scientific definition of the sphere, which Pythagoras had discovered.

The question arises again: how will Philolaus' central fire apply to limiters and unlimiteds which are themselves material, plural, and arise from Nature? How will one element, fire, be described as unlimited, while presumably the other elements, water, air, earth will not, and how can the central fire, as an element, hold sway over unlimiteds and limiters which are not only material, but undefined and unspecified originating principles? On this view, Philolaus' plural and material, originating, limiters and unlimiteds simply cannot be reduced to "a sphere," a "central fire" or a single "hearth" because limiters and unlimiteds require a harmonia to allow their inclusion into the world order.

Unlike Aristotle, who has clearly defined limiters as time, breath, and void, and leaving aside the fact that Huffman, speculating, has turned them into their opposites, namely unlimiteds, Philolaus' limiters and unlimiteds are material in nature, and as such, rather than create a world, they are subject to the laws of nature: laws of generation, day and night, the four seasons, life and death. By themselves limiters and unlimiteds can create nothing! In fact, as noted, they are incapable of making a world. A third musical factor, the harmonia, (which we will discuss later) must be called upon to allow these two opposing groups of multiple principles to join together—and if they were to join together, what would they produce? Philolaus leaves people to speculate individually upon that for themselves, as he has not said what he *meant* by *unlimiteds* and *limiters,* nor did he give any example of them.

We must extend the same judgment against the counter-earth, since it, too, is defined as invisible. Looking at the diagram of Philolaus' astronomical system (see page 90), we see the central fire at the exact center, and the counter-earth orbiting the central fire (along with other heavenly bodies depicted in the diagram).

I must confess I am somewhat amazed that in the twenty-first century, serious scholars and historians still refer, with a straight face, to Philolaus' astronomical system. Because it is quite clear, from a scientific standpoint, that there is no justification for claiming that planets and other heavenly bodies orbit an invisible and undefined something, let alone an invisible and undefined quasi-element of fire. One can to some degree nod one's head along with Burkert who described such a system as "mythology in sheep's clothing." Such a system is based on speculative dreams, not on science, astronomy, or mathematics.

If there is no mathematical or scientific definition of the central fire, then there is no possible way to conform the orbits of any planets to that central fire, since no scientist would know exactly where it was located in the heavens. It is surprising, therefore, to note that Huffman states, for Philolaus, that the Moon orbits the Earth in approximately one month, and that the Sun orbits the central fire in approximately a year—statements that under normal circumstances would apply (within our present, Copernican planetary system) to the *Sun*, and not to the central fire. (As we know, it is the *Earth* that orbits the Sun in one year.)

The same judgments may be made about the counter-earth. It is claimed that the Pythagoreans had only nine bodies in their astronomical system, and that they arbitrarily added the counter-earth to bring the total to ten in order that this total would correspond with their a priori doctrines concerning the universe.

Have we not seen enough evidence of Pythagoras' scientific and astronomical achievements, based on *exacting* mathematical reasoning, to realize that statement must be patently false? Unless physicists apply impeccable mathematical methods to their hypotheses about the universe, there is no guarantee of a proof, either for themselves or for other scientists who wish to confirm it. On the other hand, Huffman describes the system of Philolaus as "not a mathematically sophisticated account" of planetary motion, and Philolaus as a person *interested* in mathematics and not a mathematician himself. When one adds to this the general notion of the Presocratics groping, often in the dark, toward a definition of the material origin of our cosmos, it would appear that it was the Presocratics, not the Pythagoreans, who had a somewhat fantastical notion of the cosmos.

In the end, what we know of these two "heavenly bodies"—the central fire and the counter-earth—categorically dooms Philolaus' grand effort, as Huffman describes it, to provide the "most impressive example of Presocratic speculative astronomy and (as that which) establishes Philolaus as an important precursor of Plato" (ibid., 241).

HARMONIA

It may seem counterintuitive to discuss the question of the harmonia under the heading of Astronomy, but as Huffman states early on, although not a mathematician, Philolaus' purpose was to apply the harmonia to his planetary system. Therefore, it cannot be ignored.

We can contextualize this discussion by bearing in mind that in the very early days of Western scientific investigation, the main aim of the Presocratics was to search for the material origins of the cosmos. Therefore hypotheses were developed that would carry that objective forward. On the other hand, Pythagoras sought to understand the cosmos from the viewpoint of mathematics. For Philolaus, despite the hypotheses concerning the central fire and the counter-earth, his supposedly originating, multiple groups of material "principles" were unlimiteds and limiters. Huffman tells us that he never explained what these terms meant, nor did he give any example of them. As we have seen in the chapter entitled Harmonia, he describes some of them as "like" and in harmony with the world order, and others as "unlike" and needing to be brought into that harmony. Fragment 6 tells us that "it would have been impossible for them (limiteds and unlimiteds) to be ordered if a harmony had not come upon them, *in whatever way it came to be.*"

What we interpret from this last statement is that until he adopted Pythagoras' *harmonia,* or octave, consisting of the *pleasing* musical intervals of the perfect fifth and perfect fourth Philolaus had no idea how a harmony, of unknown origin, would "supervene" upon two unknown, material, and opposing groups of principles.

However, after Huffman had introduced the concept of harmonia in fragment 6 he immediately goes on to discuss it in quantitative terms (he refers to its size!) and that turns upon a discussion of the system of whole-number ratios that determine the diatonic scale. "In fact, the first actual numbers we meet in the fragments of Philolaus are this system of ratios that is said to determine the size of the *harmonia of the cosmos*" (ibid., 73). This is a remarkable statement in light of Testimoniam A24 which says the text "*plausibly* shows that he (Philolaus) knew the musical proportions (12, 9, 8, 6) which in turn *presupposes* knowledge of the arithmetic and harmonic means" (ibid., 167).

As to this last quotation, it appears that Huffman is quite unsure of what mathematics Philolaus was capable of. He *assumes*, without evidence, that Philolaus knew the mathematical ratios that supported the diatonic scale, and that he had the scientific, mathematical, and astronomical skills to *apply* this harmonia to the entire universe. Under the circumstances, that does appear to be more a Presocratic dream than a scientific possibility.

There is an additional concern. The harmonia has a *musical* source; it comprises the octave (2:1); the perfect fifth (3:2), and the perfect fourth (4:3). The harmonia does not, therefore, fit into Presocratic doctrines dealing with material origins of the cosmos. Philolaus appears to violate Presocratic doctrines of what constitutes limiteds and unlimiteds as quantitative, and redefines Aristotle's limiters as an unlimited "continuum." The art of music is the least "earthbound" of all the arts, and its purpose would diminish if we were to assign it a material origin, a Presocratic origin. For Philolaus, however, the unlimiteds and limiters would never come together unless a third principle, a *harmonia, fitted* them together, and bound them into a "world order." Is it a coincidence, then, when Nicomachus of Gerasa states that the octave—the ancient term for harmonia—was so called because it was the first concord (octave) *fitted together* from concords (perfect fourth and perfect fifth). One wonders whether Philolaus applied Pythagoras' concept of "fitting together" musical concords to his own hypothesis regarding the entire cosmos using limiters and unlimiteds as his "concords."

Huffman reminds us that it was *plausible* to see the undefined continuum of possible musical pitches as the unlimited, and that the limiters would be the boundaries we establish in this continuum by picking out specific pitches. Huffman also makes clear that it was Philolaus' intention to apply this musical model to the cosmos and that due to this achievement, he would be the first to apply mathematical solutions to philosophical problems!

In fact, the Philolaic harmonia, when applied to *unknown* material limiters and unlimiteds is an artificial construct aiming to bridge the doctrines of two different schools of thought "when applied to the universe." Considering the fact that *undefined* limiters and unlimiteds arise from and are part of the structure of Nature in Philolaus' philosophy, and that without the introduction of the third factor, the harmonia, limiters and unlimiteds would never *be* part of the world order, the Presocratic doctrines are violated by the introduction of a mathematical, musical, a priori, third term, the harmonia, a discovery made by Pythagoras. Therefore, Philolaus' introduction of the harmonia is obviously not an original discovery by him, but is, again, something he learned about and adapted from *Pythagoras.*

Furthermore, *Pythagoras* was the first to apply the harmonia to the structure of our universe in his misunderstood doctrine of the harmony of the spheres. Considering the immense difficulty, and the mystery of this hypothesis, one that vexes scholars to this day, no serious scientist could believe that Philolaus, who was not a mathematician but who had *plenty of interest* in mathematics, was the first to discover it and to announce it to the world!

Philolaus' harmonia is a novel attempt to cobble together a new and interesting (one might say fantastical) planetary system, but his musical harmonia cannot be applied to the cosmos due to a simple fact: *neither the unlimited nor the limited, nor the distances between the planets in the solar system have been scientifically defined, measured, or described!* Philolaus was not a mathematician or an astronomer, and his system is nothing short of a fairytale. A fantasy based on the mathematical and astronomical discoveries of Pythagoras!

To sum up, under his designation as a Pythagorean, Philolaus' hypotheses are shown not to be original, but are plagiarized from Pythagoras and then adapted to Presocratic purposes. As a Presocratic scientist/philosopher, he does not satisfy Presocratic scientific guidelines regarding the origins of our material world. Since he has provided no ground for his originating causes (limiters and unlimiteds) other than vague Nature, and no definitive application or proof of his inquiries, we must assume his entire planetary project regarding the central fire, counter-earth, limiters and unlimiteds to have been a doomed attempt to apply Pythagoras' mathematical doctrines to his partial *non-material* Presocratic conception of the cosmos.

PHILOLAUS' PLANETARY SYSTEM

The crucial question is: *Does* Philolaus' system square with the obvious phenomena? If we review the planetary diagram from Huffman's book (page 90) we see only five inhabitants: Sun, Moon, Earth, counter-earth, and central fire. The rest is left blank. And when we compare Philolaus' system to that of Aristotle, admittedly one hundred and fifty years later, we see a system where all the blanks have been filled in (diagram page 92). We might note that beyond the sphere of the fixed stars, Aristotle has placed the Prime Mover, God, and when adding up his number of components, with Earth at the center, the total is ten.

We have been told how critical Aristotle was of the Pythagoreans for adding the counter-earth to their planetary system merely because the other components of the system did not add up to ten, their number of perfection. Recognizing that the Prime Mover does not exist in Philolaus' schema, when *adding in* the central fire and the counter-earth to the five planets (not specified), plus Sun, Moon, Earth the number of components turns out to be eleven, a fact that should make us ponder anew as to how it ever became understood as a *Pythagorean* system.

We need to investigate Philolaus' system more fully, and will proceed by highlighting each phrase, then commenting on it afterward.

"Ten bodies circle around the central fire" (diagram, page 90). We have dealt elsewhere with the issue of the central fire, but let us note here that it is an element, the *quasi*-element of fire, and Philolaus could not possibly *locate* the center of the universe nor place the central fire there because it is *invisible*. Bluntly stated, it is impossible for ten planets to orbit an invisible concept of fire.

"Starting from the outside there are the fixed stars." Nowhere in the fragments does it say *Philolaus* investigated the heavens and reported his findings. In fact as we have noted, there are only two fragments referring to cosmology, and applied also to astronomy. In addition all of the material in the section on astronomy is taken from Aristotle or other doxographers in the ancient world, a fact that should give us serious pause, since most were followers of Aristotle or lived centuries afterward.

"...followed by five planets [no specified order], the Sun, the Moon, the Earth, and finally the counter-earth" (ibid., 244: Text 7; the Sun as seventh from the outside, Text 3). The glaring issue here is that Philolaus has not even mentioned the *names* of the planets, and therefore has no idea of their order in the planetary system. We note here that according to Heath, *Pythagoras* was the first to place the planets in the order we recognize today. "Philolaus can be seen as adopting the spherical shape for the cosmos which was probably first clearly set out by Parmenides." As Heath attests, it was *Pythagoras* who first discovered the spherical shape of the cosmos—and of the planets—but he tells us that Thales, who had also journeyed to Egypt but who had a rudimentary knowledge of their mathematics, was first to "set it out" publicly.

"The Earth is the second body out from the center, after the counter-earth." Philolaus is telling us that, except for the counter-earth, the Earth is the planet closest to the Sun. It must be obvious: If that were the case, the Earth would, like Icarus, have immediately burned up and been incinerated owing to its proximity to the raging heat of the central fire, the fire "at the center of the cosmos."

"However we never see either the central fire nor the counter-earth." The reason the central fire and the counter-earth cannot be seen is because they are *invisible*, and therefore *cannot* conform to the scientific designation of planets.

"...because the Earth rotates once on its axis as it orbits around the central fire..." Here, one intuits some confusion regarding Philolaus' system and that of Aristotle's historically accepted system. How would Philolaus *know* that the Earth rotates once on its axis as it orbits the central fire since it is invisible, and even its supposed location at the center cannot be verified? Of course we know today that the *Earth orbits the Sun* in twenty-four hours (a single diurnal rotation of its orbit), and in the ancient past, when it was commonly believed that the Earth was at the center of the cosmos, the Sun rotated around the *Earth* in one diurnal revolution. Obviously the time frame of one rotation would be less applicable to the central fire as center, than to our Earth's single diurnal rotation around the Sun!

"...thus keeping one side of the Earth always turned away from the center." Even though day and night invariably succeed one another, there is no time when "one side of the Earth is "*always* turned away from the center." From a scientific point of view, that is pure nonsense.

"...all of the bodies moving around the central fire have one circular motion from west to east." This would be true if the planets were orbiting the Sun.

"The Earth's motion is far faster than the Moon, Sun, and five planets since it completes its circuit around the central fire in twenty-four hours." First, as mentioned, if the Earth's motion were faster than the Moon or Sun, it would have been incinerated by the central fire. The notion of a twenty-four-hour orbit being coincidentally the same as the Sun around the Earth in ancient times has already been mentioned. However, Philolaus *cannot know* that Earth's orbit is faster than the five planets because he has not discovered or *described any* of the other planets and therefore could not know which was closer to the central fire and perhaps had a faster orbit. (For example, we now know that the planet Mercury's orbit takes 88 days, Venus 225 days, Mars 687 days, Jupiter 12 years, Saturn 29 years, and the fixed stars, owing to precession, approximately 26,000 years.)

"Its motion thus accounts for the *apparent movement of the Sun* across the sky (and hence for night and day) as well as the apparent nightly movement of the Moon, stars and planets from east to west." If the Earth is third out from the central fire, how could it possibly be responsible for the apparent movement of the Sun, (which is seventh out) as well as all the other planets? What is the role of the central fire if not to orchestrate the planets?

"The Earth's orbit is inclined to that of the Sun, Moon, and planets, and this inclination accounts for the apparent movement of the Sun higher and lower in the sky and hence accounts for the seasons." If it were the case that Earth's orbit was inclined to Sun, Moon and planets, it's inclination would be *away* from the central fire, turning its back to the center, as it were. And it risks being in contention *as* the center since all the planets as well as Sun and Moon are said to be included within its inclination. This is one of the more fantastical hypotheses in Philolaus planetary system. But another follows on its heels.

"The movement of the counter-earth is not made clear, but *presumably,* since its name suggests that it is paired with the Earth, it moves at a similar velocity and at the same angle to the plane of motion of the Sun and other planets." There is no scientific basis for Philolaus or Huffman *presuming* that the counter-earth is paired with Earth. Philolaus' fragments make no mention of it. Nor is there any scientific justification for presuming that it moves at a *similar velocity* as the Earth, "or at the same angle to the motion of the Sun and other planets." One wonders: Was that a Freudian slip, mentioning the Sun and other planets as though it were the *Sun* to which the counter-earth is inclined?

One important point needs to be made here. Philolaus apparently indicates that the Earth never sees either the central fire nor the counter-earth because the Earth rotates once on its axis as it orbits the central fire, and that one side of the Earth is always turned away from the center. Taking a hypothetical case, if the counter-earth were not constantly blocking the Earth, the Earth *would "see"* the central fire, so to speak. But since the counter-earth is also invisible, it would not be in the realm of physics that the counter-earth could *block* the Earth from access to the central fire. And, of course, the central fire itself is also invisible. It would not be in the grand plan of the heavens to have a "planet" such as counter-earth which *exactly* matches the orbit of another planet such as Earth. That scenario simply does not exist in the world of physics. And, if the counter-earth blocks access of the Earth to the central fire, does it not do the same to the Sun, for example, and the rest of the planets when their orbits make astronomical/astrological aspects with the counter-earth?

"The Sun, Moon, and planets then have one circular motion from west to east which is much slower (in angular velocity at least) than that of the Earth, and which explains their observed motion from west to east through the zodiac." To reiterate, the planet Mercury has an orbit of 88 days, Venus 225 days, Mars 687 days, Jupiter 12 years, Saturn 29 years, and the fixed stars, owing to precession, approximately 26,000 years. A question remains: How can Philolaus confidently assume that the Earth takes twenty-four hours to orbit the central fire? The Moon takes a month around the Earth, and the Sun a year. Today, those orbits are adjusted to our *Sun* as the center of the cosmos. Surely, if there were another center of the cosmos (in this case the central fire), the orbits should take different time periods of orbit from the planetary system we have inherited. In the case of the Sun, in the ancient world it would have been determined that it orbited *the Earth as center* not the central fire, in a year. The time frames of the planetary orbits are too conveniently based upon the orbits with which we are familiar, and when we consider that apart from the counter-earth, the Earth was closest to the central fire and its orbit fastest, it is clear that Earth would have been destroyed by the central fire and thus the whole planetary system would have collapsed. To conclude, in my view, Philolaus' system is a fanciful dream more than a serious, scientific effort to describe the cosmos that we know. As such, it was doomed to failure.

11

CONCLUSIONS

My conclusions regarding Pythagoras himself, and also Philolaus, are as follows: 1) As Thomas Heath tells us, "the subjects of which he [Pythagoras] treats become sciences *for the first time*" (Heath, *Aristarchus,* 45). As well as theoretical geometry and the theory of Numbers; he was "also the inventor of the science of acoustics [and] an astronomer of great originality." The references to these achievements can be found in chapter 2, and they speak for themselves. However, we must add to these discoveries his remarkable achievement in music! It is worth reporting Heath's findings:

> The epoch-making discovery that musical tones depend on numerical proportions, the octave representing the proportion of 2:1; the fifth 3:2; and the fourth 4:3, may with sufficient certainty be attributed to Pythagoras himself; as may the first exposition of the theory of *means,* and of *proportions* in general applied to commensurable quantities, i.e. those quantities the ratio between which can be expressed as a ratio between whole numbers. The all-pervading character of number being thus shown, what wonder that the Pythagoreans came to declare that number is the essence of all things? The connection so discovered between number and music would also lead not unnaturally to the idea of the harmony of the heavenly bodies. (ibid., 46–47)

I would add that it is also crucial to recall that the heliocentric theory of our cosmos—which Pythagoras discovered in the sixth century BC—depends for its very *foundation* upon the musical intervals mentioned.

To give a brief historical perspective, before Pythagoras, Greek music rested upon a seven-note scale played on a seven-string lyre. Pythagoras revolutionized Greek music by adding an eighth string to the lyre and, seeking "a more varied system," created a new octave that consisted of a fifth and a fourth placed side by side, a situation that made the prior extremes "produce more satisfying consonances, the octave ratio 2:1." The introduction of this fundamental change, from a seven-note system to an eight-note system, and the corresponding change to an eight-string lyre, in my view, are signs of a major evolution, not only of Greek music, but of Western consciousness itself. Howard Goodall, the internationally acclaimed musicologist reveals that the full and "dazzling fruits of this music would lie many centuries in the future."

2) The paradigm-shifting discoveries of Pythagoras inspire both awe and wonder in the discerning reader. As Édouard Schuré puts it:

> From a higher point of view, when opened with the keys of comparative esotericism, his doctrines present a magnificent composite, a solid whole, whose parts are bound by a fundamental concept. In it we find a rational reproduction of the esoteric doctrine of India and Egypt, to which he gave clarity and Hellenistic simplicity, adding a more forceful feeling and a more exact idea of human freedom.
>
> At the same time, and in various parts of the globe, great reformers were making similar doctrines more generally known. These include Lao-Tse in China; the last Buddha, Shakyamuni, in India; King Numa in Rome, Italy.... And it is not by chance that these great reformers appear at the same time among such different peoples. Their varied missions are united in a common goal. They prove that at certain times a single spiritual current mysteriously passes through all humankind. Where does it come from? From that divine world which is beyond our sight, but whose seers and prophets are its ambassadors and witnesses.*

Schuré reveals that Pythagoras should be included among those with a divine mission to further the evolution of humanity.

---

* See Schuré, *The Great Initiates*, pp. 269.

3) As to the position of Philolaus within the Pythagorean and the Presocratic traditions, as championed by Carl Huffman, it is impossible to imagine that someone who was not a mathematician, but had *plenty of interest* in mathematics, could reasonably be expected to have displaced the Earth from the center of the cosmos in favor of the *invisible* central fire and counter-earth, *non-scientific* principles, which have no shred of evidence in their favor. Nor could Philolaus possibly be named as a precurser to Plato. The idea is preposterous.

In my view Philolaus was essentially a Presocratic. Even Carl Huffman places the "cosmology" of Philolaus among the Presocratics, telling us that his planetary system "has been subject to the widest range of assessments imaginable, but the true nature of its contribution to the development of *Presocratic* thought has seldom been appreciated" (Huffman, 240). This statement is surprising when we consider that Philolaus had only two fragments (7 and 17) that applied to both cosmology *and* astronomy. Nevertheless, it seems Philolaus was somehow connected with the Pythagoreans. If Philolaus was indeed the head of a Pythagorean group in Thebes, the instruction given by him bore absolutely no semblance to the original metaphysical doctrines of Pythagoras as laid out in the Alexander Polyhistor template. The examples of Cebes and Simmias, supposed Pythagoreans quizzed by Socrates in Plato's *Phaedo* dialogue (84c–88b), who no longer had any belief in the immortality of the soul, confirm that, in some quarters following the death of Pythagoras himself, his teachings had indeed become changed by time and the vagaries of human nature and history.

After reviewing all the material in this book, I reiterate my view that Philolaus was essentially a Presocratic, but it is also my view that Philolaus was privy to some of Pythagoras' secret doctrines, including the heliocentric theory and that of the harmony of the spheres, as well as most of his scientific, mathematical, geometric, musical, and astronomical discoveries. It is my further judgment that he plagiarized most of these features from Pythagoras and adapted them to reveal a new and marvelous heavenly creation—a quasi *Presocratic* creation—which, as Armitage tells us, "never established itself." All this implies that Philolaus was not part of those disciples who kept faith with Pythagoras' instruction that these doctrines were to be kept secret from the public. For authentic and true disciples of Pythagoras we wait for such as Iamblichus and Porphyry who appeared in the third century AD.

JUDGMENT

We might wonder: What was the *reason* behind Philolaus' actions? One answer is offered by Iamblichus in his *Life of Pythagoras* (reproduced in Guthrie's *Pythagorean Sourcebook and Library*). It reads as follows: "For during so many centuries, prior to the times of Philolaus, none of the Pythagorean commentaries appeared publicly. Philolaus first published those three celebrated books, which, at the request of Plato, Dion of Syracuse is said to have bought for a hundred minae. For Philolaus had been overtaken by sudden severe poverty, and he *capitalized the writings of which he was partaker through his alliance* with the Pythagoreans."

Three consequences follow: 1) Philolaus was *allied* only with the Pythagoreans; 2) he broke their sacred vow of silence—observed for several centuries—regarding publication of the doctrines and commentaries; and 3) he betrayed Pythagoras for money.

Bibliography

Armitage, Angus. *Copernicus: The Founder of Modern Astronomy.* Plainsboro, NJ: Thomas Yoseloff, 1957.

Burkert, Walter. *Lore and Science in Ancient Pythagoreanism.* Cambridge, MA: Harvard University, 1972.

Burn, A. R. (ed.). *Herodotus: The Histories* (tr. A. de Selincourt). New York: Penguin, 1964

Burnet, John. *Early Greek Philosophy.* London: Adam and Black, 1948.

Caspar, Max. *Kepler.* New York: Dover, 1993.

Clark, Gillian. *Iamblichus: On the Pythagorean Life.* Liverpool, UK: Liverpool University, 1989.

Cooper, John M. (ed.). *Plato: Complete Works.* Indianapolis: Hackett, 1997.

Cornford, F. M. *From Religion to Philosophy.* London: Harper, 1957.

Curd, Patricia (ed.). *A Presocratics Reader: Selected Fragments and Testimonia.* Indianapolis: Hackett. 1996.

de Santillana, Georgio. *The Crime of Galileo.* Chicago: University of Chicago, 1955.

———. *Reflections on Men and Ideas.* Cambridge, MA: MIT, 1968.

Diels, Hermann (ed.). *Doxographi Graeci.* Cambridge, UK: Cambridge University, 2010.

Dillon, John M. *Iamblichi Chalcidensis in Platonis Dialogos Commentariorum Fragmenta: Iamblichus, the Platonic Commentaries.* Leiden, Netherlands: Brill, 1973.

Dreyer, J. L. E. *A History of Astronomy from Thales to Kepler.* New York: Dover 1953.

Fideler, David. *The Pythagorean Sourcebook and Library.* Grand Rapids, MI: Phanes, 1987.

Godwin, Joscelyn. *The Harmony of the Spheres: A Sourcebook of the Pythagorean Tradition in Music.* Rochester, VT: Inner Traditions, 1992.

Guthrie, Kenneth Sylvan (ed.). *The Pythagorean Sourcebook and Library: An Anthology of Ancient Writings which Relate to Pythagoras and Pythagorean Philosophy.* Grand Rapids, MI: Phanes, 1988.

Guthrie, W. K. C. *The Greek Philosophers: From Thales to Aristotle.* New York: Harper, 1950.

———. *A History of Greek Philosophy,* vol. 1. Cambridge, UK: Cambridge University, 1950, 1975.

Hadas, M. and M. Smith. *Heroes and Gods: Spiritual Biographies in Antiquity, Porphry's Life of Pythagoras.* New York: Harper, 1965.

Hamilton, E., and H. Cairns (eds.). *Plato: Collected Dialogues.* Princeton, NJ: Princeton University, 1961.

Heath, Sir Thomas. *Aristarchus of Samos: The Ancient Copernicus.* New York: Dover, 2004.

———. *A History of Greek Mathematics, Volume 1: The Earlier Presocratics and the Pythagoreans.* Cambridge, UK: Cambridge University, 1971.

Hemenway, Priya. *Divine Proportion: Phi in Art, Nature, and Science.* New York: Sterling, 2005.

Huffman, Carl A. *Philolaus of Croton: Pythagorean and Presocratic.* Cambridge, UK: Cambridge University, 1993.

Iamblichus. *On the Pythagorean Life* (tr. G. Clark). Liverpool: Liverpool University, 1989.

Kahn, Charles. *Pythagoras and the Pythagoreans: A Brief History.* Indianapolis: Hackett, 2001.

Kepler, Johannes. *Harmonies of the World.* New York: Prometheus Books, 1955.

Laertius, Diogenes. *Lives of Eminent Philosophers,* vol 2 (tr. R. D. Hicks). Cambridge, MA: Harvard University, 1925.

Levin, Flora R. *The Manual of Harmonics of Niccomachus the Pythagorean.* Grand Rapids, MI: Phanes, 1994.

Lockyer, J. Norman. *The Dawn of Astronomy.* New York: Dover, 2006.

McKeon, Richard. *The Basic Works of Aristotle.* New York, Random House, 1941.

Oldfather, C. H. *Diodorus of Sicily,* vol. 4. Cambridge, UK: Cambridge University, 1946.

———. (ed., tr.). *Diodorus Siculus: Diodorus of Sicily,* vol 1. Cambridge, MA: Harvard University, 1936.

Philip, J. A. *Pythagoras and Early Pythagoreanism.* Toronto: University of Toronto, 1996.

Schuré, Édouard. *The Great Initiates: A Study of the Secret History of Religions.* Great Barrington, MA: SteinerBooks, 1992.

Taylor, A. E. *Plato: The Man and his Work.* New York: Meridian, 1952.

A Note from SteinerBooks

SteinerBooks is a 501 (c)(3) not-for-profit organization, incorporated in New York State since 1928 to promote the progress and welfare of humanity and to increase public awareness of Rudolf Steiner (1861–1925), the Austrian-born polymath writer, lecturer, spiritual scientist, philosopher, cosmologist, educator, psychologist, alchemist, ecologist, Christian mystic, comparative religionist, and evolutionary theorist, who was the creator of Anthroposophy ("human wisdom") as a path uniting the spiritual in the human being with the spiritual in the universe; and to this end publish and distribute books for adults and children, utilize the electronic media, hold conferences, and engage in similar activities making available his works and exploring themes arising from, and related to, them and the movement that he founded.

- We commission translations of books by Rudolf Steiner unpublished in English, as well as new translations for updated editions.

- Our aim is to make works on Anthroposophy available to all by publishing and distributing both introductory and advanced works on spiritual research.

- New books are publish for both print and digital editions to reach the widest possible readership.

- Recent technology also makes it efficient for us to make our previously out-of-print works available for the next generation.

SteinerBooks depends on our readers' financial support, which is greatly needed, appreciated, and tax-deductible. Please consider a donation by check or other means to SteinerBooks, 610 Main St., Great Barrington, MA 01230. We also accept donations via PayPal on our website. For more information about supporting our work, send email to friends@steinerbooks.org or call 413-528-8233.